SOUTHERN LITERARY CLASSICS SERIES

C. Hugh Holman and Louis D. Rubin, Jr.
General Editors

Previously published:

CHITA, *by Lafcadio Hearn, introduction by Arlin Turner, Duke University*

IN OLE VIRGINIA, *by Thomas Nelson Page, introduction by Kimball King, The University of North Carolina at Chapel Hill*

ADVENTURES OF CAPTAIN SIMON SUGGS, *by Johnson Jones Hooper, introduction by Manly Wade Wellman*

TIGER-LILIES, *by Sidney Lanier, introduction by Richard Harwell, Smith College*

THE PLANTER'S NORTHERN BRIDE, *by Caroline Lee Hentz, introduction by Rhoda Coleman Ellison*

In preparation:

THE VALLEY OF SHENANDOAH, *by George Tucker, introduction by Donald R. Noble, University of Alabama*

THE KNIGHTS OF THE GOLDEN HORSE-SHOE, *by William Alexander Caruthers, introduction by Curtis Carroll Davis*

THE PARTISAN LEADER, *by Nathaniel Beverley Tucker, introduction by C. Hugh Holman, The University of North Carolina at Chapel Hill*

THE LETTERS OF THE BRITISH SPY

THE LETTERS
OF THE BRITISH SPY

by
WILLIAM WIRT, ESQ.

to which is prefixed
A Biographical Sketch of the Author

With an Introduction by

RICHARD BEALE DAVIS

THE UNIVERSITY OF NORTH CAROLINA PRESS
Chapel Hill

The 1832 edition used in duplicating this work is in the Virginia State Library, Richmond, Virginia.

INTRODUCTION

In the late summer of 1803 a thirty-year-old Virginia lawyer, absent from his family on professional business, sat down in his tavern room in Richmond and began penning a series of prose sketches. He was attempting to take his mind off certain pressing legal problems and his anxiety at his wife's approaching confinement in Norfolk, then his place of residence. The resulting ten essays were published in a local newspaper, the *Virginia Argus*, and were dated from September 1 through December 10, though all appeared in August and September issues. In October or November the first book edition appeared, followed immediately by a second edition in December, both bearing Richmond imprints. In 1804 an edition was brought out in Newburyport, Massachusetts; another in 1805 (reprinted in 1808) in Richmond; at least six (in nine or more separate printings) in Baltimore from 1811; one in London in 1812; and eight or nine issues of a tenth edition in New York between 1832 and 1875. In the Philadelphia Federalist magazine the *Port Folio*, 1804 and 1805, an imitation, and in one instance a burlesque, "The British Spy in Boston," ran in six issues. On the frontier, at Rogersville in Tennessee, *The Englishman; or, Letters Found in the State of Tennessee, Supposed To Be the Production of an Eng-*

lishman, Travelling through the United States as a Spy,
was printed in 1815. And there were other imitations.

No one was more surprised than the author at the
enormous popularity of what he considered the desultory
productions of idle hours. Within the next decade he was
to compose better essays for the *Rainbow* (1804) and *Old
Bachelor* (1814) series, and in 1817 he was to publish his
Sketches of the Life and Character of Patrick Henry with
the famous "orations" attributed to his subject but molded
by Wirt himself from bits and pieces of myths and memories. It was in *The British Spy*, however, that the quondam
rollicking lawyer first made a place for himself in the literature of his period and established the first Southern reputation in belles-lettres.

The Letters of the British Spy is clearly a product of
its time and place. It is, in form, in the tradition of Mon-
tesquieu's *Les Lettres Persanes* (1721), Walpole's *Letters
from Xo-Ho* (1757), Lyttleton's *Letters from a Persian in
England* (2nd ed., 1735), and Goldsmith's *Citizen of the
World; or, Letters from a Chinese Philosopher* (1760) as
well as the American Benjamin Silliman's *Letters of Shah-
coolen* (1802) and the later satirical Turkish letters in
Irving's *Salmagundi* (1807) or Ingersoll's *Inchiquin's
Letters* (1810). The letter forms in the *Spectator* are less
evident as models than are other aspects of that periodical.
In style and spirit Wirt employs the *Spectator* in shaping
a prose anticipating Irving's *Sketch Book* and Hawthorne's
non-fictional or semi-fictional essays. It is patriotically
American, particularly Virginian and Southern, even in its
mild strictures. It ponders Virginia's (and for Virginia's
one may read most of the Old South's) declining part in
the shaping of the nation. Jefferson had several more years
in the presidency, and he was to be followed by his fellow-
Virginians Madison and Monroe. But Wirt felt that no new

generation equal to the Revolutionary giants was coming along which might fill their places. In an age and in a region where the law was the path to prominence, he was attempting to show how an able new generation might be produced.

In doing so he was employing the form of the familiar essay, most popular in Virginia and the colonies generally since the first gazettes had been established in the early eighteenth century. From its beginning in the 1730's contributors to the *Virginia Gazette* had often employed the letter form. The Carters, Blands, and Randolphs had used it for a variety of purposes, including economic, political, and religious, and frequently as strong polemics. Wirt, here alone and later with a circle of friends, Southern urbanites, and country gentlemen, continued and extended this familiar essay tradition. There were now no problems of such specific immediacy as British tyranny or constitutional government, but there was the problem of the future of the oldest and most opulent commonwealth.

Wirt considered one key to the situation to be the state of eloquence or oratory, political and legal. He is critically suggestive, by contemporary example and direct discussion, of what the rising Virginia generation, aided by its elders, must do if the Old Dominion is to retain or regain her leadership in the nation. His suggestions are made in the frame of reference of Virginia's past history and of its indifference to present needs in education and incentive for youth. Other topics reflecting the interests of the age and of the man are also touched upon.

Wirt's avowed aims were to present a picture of his state in his time and to offer guidance to its youth. In both these he anticipated the themes of both his later essays and of his life of Patrick Henry, thus anticipating one tradition in Southern writing which has endured to our own time. For consciously and unconsciously, through George W. Bagby and Ellen Glasgow to William Faulkner, the South has been and is concerned, even obsessed, with its place in contemporary America, the meaning and significance of its own past, and the future of its people.

The *Spy*'s national reputation in Wirt's time came in part because the rest of the United States wanted to see what Virginia, still its leader, thought of itself. Perhaps in doing so these outsiders found criteria by which to judge themselves. The rest of the country also had a proprietary interest in Wirt's subjects—America's past in relation to its present, the desperate need for the support of education in the new republic, and above all the nature of and the great examplars of forensic eloquence. And his outspoken condemnation of Godwinism, deism, and atheism agreed with the growing sentiment of the period of the second Great Awakening.

The themes of *The British Spy* would of themselves never have brought the popularity the book attained if there had not been a pleasing style, the good-natured satirical touched with the moral, the combination of the rational and sensibility—as Wirt called them—or the head and the heart. For Wirt's mixture of the logical plain-style with soaring rhetoric, of the homely and the sublime, was a fusion of older forms and tones with newer romantic attitudes.

The British Spy was recognized at once as a transparent alias for a native American and Virginian, though Wirt tried with some success to have his letter-writer see and describe only what a casual visitor in Jefferson's Old Dominion would have had the opportunity and the ability to observe and understand. Letter I is a mild criticism of the Virginia socioeconomic system through observations of the inequality of land distribution, the contrast between stately mansions and crude huts in a belated feudalism in this

land of "equal liberty and equal rights." The debasing
sense of inferiority the poorer classes were compelled to
feel is presented alongside a scathing denunciation of Virginia's recent fawning hospitality to the boorish son of the
last royal governor, Lord Dunmore, though asterisks re-
place names.

From this condemnation of snobbery the Spy turns to
a description of Richmond and a brief account of its found-
ing by William Byrd and of that gentleman's adventures
in running the boundary line between Virginia and North
Carolina. Obviously the writer has seen at least portions of
Byrd's famous "History of the Dividing Line" in the
original or in someone's copy, and he mentions in a note
that the manuscript account is still in the Byrd family, interesting evidence that the Southern classic circulated in
manuscript among Virginians long before it first appeared
in print in 1841, years after Wirt's death.[1] This almost
incidental reference suggests a great deal about the knowledge and reading of Southern-authored manuscript works
well into the national period and the general awareness of
Byrd's writing generations before it appeared in print.[2]

1. Wirt was probably referring to the family copy of the holo-
graph "History" (distinct from "The Secret History"), long in
the Byrd family and recently acquired by the Virginia Historical
Society.

2. Kathleen L. Leonard, "Notes on the Text and Provenance of
the Byrd Manuscripts," in *The Prose Works of William Byrd of
Westover*, ed. Louis B. Wright (New York, 1966), pp. 417-23, sums
up the early nineteenth-century history of the two accounts of the
Dividing Line. The American Philosophical Society, early in that
century, came into possession of a manuscript copy of "The History,"
and in 1817 Jefferson deposited the manuscript of "The Secret History" there. They—or one of them—were considered for publication
by a committee of the Society, though nothing came of the matter.
The copy Wirt knew of was probably, though not necessarily, the
third manuscript, that which came to the Virginia Historical Society
very recently. There were editions of "The History" and miscellaneous writings several times between 1841 and 1929. The first authoritative text of the two histories is that of Louis B. Wright noted

Letter II apparently provoked the most immediate controversy or rebuttal in Virginia and yet today is the least important and interesting of the ten. Wirt, who admitted to his friend Dabney Carr that he had read little and knew less of geological theory and natural history, here gave a fairly ingenious argument as to the mode of creation of the North American continent, its present and past shore lines, the origin of mountains, and the abundance of fossil remains. He cites authorities he knew only from hasty reading. The principal interest of the letter lies in the actual evidence cited of fossil discoveries along the James River and in the Blue Ridge and of the author's breadth of interests.

From the first book edition on there were included two rejoinders to this essay and its theory by "An Inquirer," one placed immediately after Letter III and the other after Letter X, though logically they should have appeared immediately after II. "An Inquirer" was George Tucker, whose scientific knowledge was far more profound and comprehensive than Wirt's. Though Tucker later was to compose, both with the Wirt circle and alone, some highly entertaining, graceful, and thoughtful essays, in these two he is merely ponderous and dull, laboriously arguing theories now long considered obvious or outmoded. Letter II and its appendices are, with certain of the writings of Jefferson, Francis Gilmer, Bishop Madison, and St. George Tucker, among the evidences of the scientific curiosity

above. Percy G. Adams has re-edited the William K. Boyd 1929 parallel-text edition of the two histories (New York, 1967). For a detailed discussion of attempts early in the nineteenth century (though long after the first edition of *The Spy*) by Jefferson and others to get the histories published, see Leonard, "Notes on the Text and Provenance of the Byrd Manuscripts" in Wright, *Prose Works*, pp. 417-22. Recently there has come to the editor's attention the fact that a few installments of "The History" appeared in the Petersburg (Va.) *Republican* of 1822.

about the nature and origin of its own good earth manifested in Virginia and the South from 1585 to the present.[3]

Letters IV, VI, and IX meditate upon Virginia's past
history, with emphasis on its significance for the present.
Letter IV was written after a morning's ride to an Indian
village, a visit that conjures up images of Pocahontas and
memories of the injustices the white man has meted out to
the red. In general the Spy agrees with Jefferson's idea of
savagism and the moral character of the Indian,[4] but he
is less rational and more sentimental than is the author of
Notes on the State of Virginia. As many a later and greater
writer has done, the Spy sees Pocahontas as a great symbol
of America's beginnings, and he wonders why a festival
has not been instituted in her honor.

In VI, sitting among the tombs near the ruined tower
of the Jamestown church, he ponders the significance of
the deserted cradle of a mighty nation. In something of
the tone of Sterne or of the author of Ossian, he enquires
about the shades of Captain John Smith and other worth-
ies. But the *ubi sunt* leads to reflections on the sickly germ
from which the great flowering plant that is the United
States has sprung. All this, though it consumes most of

3. Cf. Richard Beale Davis, *Intellectual Life in Jefferson's Virginia, 1790-1830* (Chapel Hill, 1964), pp. 147-204. For Tucker's
rejoinders and the fact that Tucker himself was believed by many
to be the author of *The Letters,* see Robert C. McLean, *George
Tucker, Moral Philosopher and Man of Letters* (Chapel Hill, 1961).
pp. 52-59. Tucker's rejoinders also appeared originally in the *Argus,*
though belatedly and therefore in the book editions placed at some
distance from what they answered. The first rejoinder appeared in
the first book edition, the second in later editions.

4. Davis, *Intellectual Life,* pp. 202-3. Throughout his life Wirt,
like Jefferson, was to show sympathy for the Indians. He distinguished himself late in his career in the litigation, Cherokee Nation
v. Georgia, in which for once he and Chief Justice Marshall agreed,
though President Andrew Jackson was much opposed. See Joseph
C. Robert, ''The Humors of a Chief Justice,'' *The Alumni Bulletin
of the University of Richmond,* XXVII (Winter, 1964), 14, 37.

xiv   INTRODUCTION

the space, is but prelude for the moral, the contrast between supreme self-sacrifice in the past and selfish material acquisitiveness in his own time. For Virginia, with all her present wealth, needs highways, public buildings, and a great university in which the young may be nurtured.

Letter IX in some respects takes up where VI leaves off, for the Spy turns specifically to the necessity of developing natural talent through education. Gray's *Elegy* is quoted to remind Wirt's readers of youthful potential wasted, and he continues by discussing the bill for the general diffusion of knowledge which Jefferson and his friends had proposed in the 1780's, a plan never adopted. Again he speaks, as in the two earlier essays of this group, of the want of public spirit. Wirt knew that the Middle and Northern states were progressing past his own at an accelerating pace, and like Jefferson he saw the key to good government, to a great future, was the cultivation of an aristocracy of virtue and talents.

Four Letters, III, V, VII, and VIII, perhaps the strongest in appealing themes and felicitous style, are all concerned with one thing several literary historians have called the real subject of the whole series—eloquence. Wirt was thoroughly aware of the golden age of great orators which had just preceded his. Like most of his contemporaries he believed that law, government, and religion were controlled or created by the force of great discourses. He cited Demosthenes and Cicero (the latter of whom he did not at this time admire), Quintilian, Chatham, and a host of other theorists and practitioners from classical antiquity to late eighteenth-century Europe. His rhetorical and critical views are largely those of Hugh Blair in his *Lectures on Rhetoric and Belles-Lettres* (1st ed., 1783), a Scottish manual of aesthetics and literary criticism which was the great textbook of the English-speaking peoples from the time of its original publication in Great Britain to the mid-nineteenth century, when Edward Tyrrel Channing of Harvard was still using it, as he had earlier used it in teaching Emerson and Lowell. Though Wirt had read and admired Burke, his idea of the sublime—or grandeur—is essentially Blair's rather than the Irishman's. Blair's demand for precision in sentence structure, his analyses of several *Spectator* essays as models of style, his insistence on nature as opposed to artifice as the basis of great oratory, were all matters Wirt referred to in his own writing throughout his life. Blair was of course the pedagogical mouthpiece of the Scottish aestheticians, the Common-Sense school, which in the years after *The British Spy* were to supply the principles on which the early American fictionalists and poets such as Poe were to construct their own theories of art, or from which they consciously departed or progressed.

Letter III comments upon the present state of eloquence in Virginia, which the Spy observes shows three great defects, want of a sufficient fund of general knowledge, of a habit of close and solid thinking, and of an aspiration "at original ornaments." For the moment the Spy holds the discussion or examples of these deficiencies in abeyance and launches into a rambling discourse on the necessity for pathos or sympathy in true oratory, a reflection of the heart more than of the head, as a means of convincing mankind. All around are men who employ cold and artificial conceits. But he has heard of one speaker of whom Virginia can boast, "the celebrated Patrick Henry," the orator of nature. For a page or two Wirt expatiates on Henry's *natural* virtues in eloquence, qualities he greatly overemphasizes both here and in his later life of Henry.

Having commented in general on Virginia oratory, in Letter V the Spy turns to specific cases. Here he considers

two representative statesmen, men who are not named but
who are easily identified, James Monroe and John Marshall.
Monroe had just completed a term as governor. Marshall
was already chief justice of the United States. Though
Wirt belonged to Monroe's Democratic-Republican political party (and was later to serve under him as attorney
general), he shows greater respect for the abilities of the
Federalist jurist. Here are two of the best contemporary
sketches of these men. They have been quoted again and
again. Both are carefully done, mildly but genuinely
critical, rational. They are more than analyses of oratorical
style, for Wirt knew that person and mind were integral to
individual oral expression, and in a series of deft strokes
he pictures each man and then examines his method in
speaking. The Spy's insights, if not profound, are shrewd
and perceptive. His style, simple and yet enforced with
paradox and an occasional striking image, enhances the
portraits and engages the attention. Only Wirt's brother-
in-law Francis Gilmer, in his 1816 *Sketches of American
Orators*, was to rival Wirt among his contemporaries in
the incisiveness of presentation of the chief justice as
speaker.

In the first months after the publication of *The Letters*
there was a running debate in newspapers of the nation
between critics and defenders of the Spy in which this
sketch of Marshall had considerable part. The chief justice is said to have taken it with good grace, though his wife
considered it an insult. In subsequent years Wirt was to
express privately to Judge Dabney Carr a far less favor-
able opinion of the great jurist, suggesting that Marshall
may even have shown a lack of probity in the famous Burr
trial. Wirt as attorney general was to become fairly intimate with the chief justice, and they are said to have admired each other. In private letters throughout his life

Wirt expressed what are on the whole sound observations on Marshall's mind and action. But here at the beginning of both his literary and legal career, Wirt caught and expressed clearly both the person and mind of John Marshall.[5]

In Letter VIII, with less discretion, the Spy examines the oratorical pretensions of two of the prominent trial lawyers of Richmond, former secretary of state Edmund Randolph and John Wickham, a somewhat younger man. Again Wirt is without political bias and as far as the sketches go apparently without personal bias. Randolph is allowed a number of strong qualities, which with pomposity, fondness for literary finery, and generally artificial manner, add up to a balanced picture of a well-informed lawyer and sometimes beautiful speaker. Wirt wrote to a friend that Randolph took offence at the portrait and vowed revenge, though nothing came of it.[6] The talents of Federalist John Wickham were presented in the *Argus* and in the first book edition with a mixture of complimentary and strongly critical analysis paralleling what Randolph was subjected to. But Wirt learned that Wickham took it very well, and in an after-note to the first book edition and later in the text of all subsequent editions the portrait of Wickham was softened into an obviously sympathetic one. Ironically enough, in later years Wickham, a staunch Federalist, opposed and attacked Wirt many times, apparently with personal animosity.

5. Wirt's mature private opinion of Marshall, expressed in a letter to Carr of December 30, 1827, seems today innocent enough; but John Pendleton Kennedy saw fit to delete it when he published other portions of the epistle in *Memoirs of the Life of William Wirt*, 2 vols. (Philadelphia, 1849; rev. ed., 1850). For a detailed and interesting study of Marshall as seen through Wirt's eyes, see Robert, "The Humors of a Chief Justice." Professor Robert, who is completing a biography of Wirt, has been most generous in sharing his knowledge on this and many other points.

6. Kennedy, *Memoirs* (1850), I, 110-11, letter of January 16, 1804.

The most famous of the letters, No. VII, read and re-
cited by schoolboys throughout much of the nineteenth
century and a favorite with clergymen, describes without
paraphrasing or quoting (except for a sentence or two) a
sermon by the Reverend James Waddell, a Presbyterian
minister Wirt makes appear less well-known than he actual-
ly was. This is the Spy's example of pulpit oratory. Sentimental and overly rhetorical in style, it appeals far less
today than the sober and rational examinations of the lawyers and statesmen. The author casts Waddell, as he did
Henry earlier and later, in the role of the orator of nature,
of the heart rather than of the head. Years later Wirt
wrote a series of ''Hints to Preachers'' for his friend John
Holt Rice's *Virginia Evangelical and Literary Magazine*
in which he expressed less sentimentally his theories as to
what pulpit eloquence might and should be. But here he
was so moved in describing a genuinely eloquent sermon
that he descants on religion with what we might consider
sentimental bathos.

Letter X, the last, is a pæan of praise of the *Spectator*,
inspired by an idle night in a wayside hostelry with one
volume of that periodical for company. Wirt's familiarity
with Addison's style, his characters, and his subjects is
evident. The Spy wishes he might present a copy of the
Spectator to every youth in the land as something that is
at once a moral guide, a literary model, and an intellectual
stimulus. He wishes he might write a philosophical history
of style in which Addison and Steele's journal would have
its proper place. But it would be a mistake to assume from
this last letter that Wirt was consciously or unconsciously
a belated American or Virginia Addison. For the essays of
The British Spy, perhaps lightened into their mild and
often playful satire by the *Spectator's* example, owe equally as much to Goldsmith and Blair in their critical prin-

ciples and general choice of subjects. In their style they
have been warmed by the pre-Romantics such as Macpher-
son and Gray and by the whimsy of Sterne. Finally, in
their immediate choice of subjects they are timely and
timelessly Virginian and Southern. For the interest in the
past, the relation to God, the love of the rhetorical flow in
communication, and the prepossession with one's country,
or region, are abiding.

This early national emanation of the Southern literary
mind came from a man of humble origins[7] who by hard
work and gay and amiable disposition climbed to the top
of the legal profession, and of the literary profession, of
his time. His tone is mild, but his criticism has its edge.
He entertained as he instructed and he wrote of a South
he knew.

In the laudatory "Advertisement" to Fielding Lucas'
Baltimore edition of 1811 (and continued in all later
editions), John E. Hall, editor of the Philadelphia *Port
Folio*, concludes that "the letters of the British Spy [are
offered] as an unquestionable evidence that America is
entitled to a high rank in the republic of letters. . . ." The
National Aegis[8] had as early as 1804 bestowed even more
lavish praise. The London edition of 1812 in a prefatory
note spoke of this "specimen of American literature highly flattering to the rising genius of that nation."

Wirt's own verdict is closer to the truth: "The letters
bespeak a mind rather frolicksome and sprightly, than
thoughtful and penetrating; and therefore a mind qualified to amuse, for the moment, but not to benefit either its
proprietor, or the world, by the depth and utility of its
researches. The style, though sometimes happy, is sometimes, also, careless and poor; and, still more frequently,

7. See biographical sketch below, immediately preceding the essays,
and Kennedy, *Memoirs*.
8. Reprinted in the *Argus*, July 11, 1804.

overloaded with epithets; and its inequality proves either that the author wanted time or industry or taste to give it, throughout, a more even tenor. Yet these letters are certainly superior to the trash with which we are so frequently gorged through the medium of the press."[9] Even so, the British Spy might have sat for George W. Bagby's portrait of the Old Virginia Gentleman or for one of those of the civilized Southern males drawn by Thomas Nelson Page or Ellen Glasgow.

9. Kennedy, *Memoirs*, I, 112, to Dabney Carr. Also in a letter to Ninian Edwards (printed in Ninian Edwards, *History of Illinois from 1778 to 1833; and Life of Ninian Edwards* [Springfield, 1870], p. 45) Wirt offers a similar estimate of *The Spy*. One of the most amusing of contemporary opinions of *The Spy* was reported by Wirt in a letter to his wife of October 11, 1803 (now in the Maryland Historical Society). He quotes the Petersburg, Virginia, firebrand, historian, and playwright John D. Burke as telling him that though Wirt had *some* talents they were not of sufficiently high order to have enabled him to have written *The Letters of the British Spy*.

BIBLIOGRAPHICAL NOTE

For more material on William Wirt as man and writer, see John P. Kennedy, *Memoirs of the Life of William Wirt*, 2 vols. (Philadelphia, 1849; rev. ed., 1850); Jay B. Hubbell, *The South in American Literature* (Durham, N.C., 1954), and "William Wirt and the Familiar Essay in Virginia," *William and Mary Quarterly*, 2nd ser., XXIII (1943), 136-52; Richard Beale Davis, *Francis Walker Gilmer: Life and Learning in Jefferson's Virginia* (Richmond, 1939), and *Intellectual Life in Jefferson's Virginia, 1790-1830* (Chapel Hill, 1964).

For editions of the present work, see B. Randolph Wellford, "Check-List of Editions of Wirt's *The Letters of the British Spy*," *Secretary's News Sheet* of the Bibliographical Society of the University of Virginia, no. 31, pp. 10-16. There are few changes between the *Virginia Argus* and the first book edition except those noted above, especially in Letter VIII. Spelling and punctuation have been somewhat modified in later editions, with the "last corrections of the author" and a few Latin phrases omitted. John E. Hall's "Advertisement" was added in the fourth edition, Baltimore, 1811, and retained in subsequent editions. Peter Hoffman Cruse's biographical sketch appeared in the 1832 first printing of the tenth edition (when Wirt was still living) and was retained in later printings through 1875.

Despite Kennedy's *Memoirs*, the publishers continued to feel rightly that here was a succinct and sympathetic but factually accurate introduction to an author and statesman who had made a great personal impression on his and the next generations. Readers who knew him by general reputation could thus become acquainted with the major details of a career the nineteenth century liked to think of as characteristically American. For the mere facts of the life showed as unmistakably as did those of Franklin's that distinction, and a major part in the building of a nation, could come from modest beginnings if one possessed the virtues of hard work, practicality, moral integrity, and energy.

It is the tenth edition, revised and corrected, that is reproduced here. The text of this volume starts with page 9 as the frontmatter of the original was numbered in Arabic numerals.

THE LETTERS OF THE BRITISH SPY

WILLIAM WIRT, ESQ.

BIOGRAPHICAL SKETCH

OF

WILLIAM WIRT.

IN reprinting a portion of the literary productions of Mr. Wirt, the publishers have thought
that a few particulars might not be unacceptable
to the reader, of an individual who has long
been familiar to the public in other positions
very different from that of the writer or mere
man of letters. They are indebted, in great
part, for the opportunity of giving these details,
to materials collected by another hand, some time
since, and for another purpose. The present
occasion may excuse a sketch which other obvious considerations, however, may render somewhat meager. Biography has a delicate office
while her subjects are yet living, as she may be
accused of flattery on the one hand, and, on the
other, may be thought to misplace and mistime
the impartial censure which she, no less than
History, owes to truth, when, like the Egyptian
tribunal, she sits in judgment on the dead.

With regard to the subject himself, the mind most conscious of integrity, and the most happy in deserved success, may naturally shrink from that scrupulous analysis which is necessary to a full delineation of it. It is as naturally averse to the relation of many things, trivial in themselves, but characteristic, and which on that account are eagerly sought when the actors are no more, though till then they may fail to excite curiosity or interest in the public. Contemporary actors have their sensibilities also; a consideration which, in tracing the competitions and conflicts through which an individual has wrought his way to honour and influence, may require many sketches to be withheld, much of the colouring softened, and much of what may be called the material action suppressed.

It is not so much the brief memoir designed in the following pages that leads to these suggestions, as the observation how often they are neglected in the license of the press and the rage of anecdote. But even in this hasty sketch, it is evident how many passages of a life somewhat various and busy, and how many incidents collected by his intimates, from an acute observer and lively describer, must thus be excluded, though at the expense of the vivacity of the

whole picture. At some future day, and by
some happier hand, a more minute delineation
might be profitably exhibited of singular merit
gradually achieving its own reward ; a career
the more interesting as descriptive of a course of
fortune familiar, though not peculiar indeed, to
our happy country, where native talent has a
fair field, and where its acquisitions of honour
are more unquestionably the fruit of its own
intrinsic vigour.

In point of pecuniary circumstances and early
education, the subject of our memoir had what
may be reckoned middling advantages, considering the aspect of our country in both particulars
at that early day. His parents left him some
patrimony, small indeed, but which was sufficient to procure him the usual instruction of the
grammar-school. He was born at Bladensburg,
in Maryland, on the 8th of November, 1772, and
was the youngest of six children of Jacob and
Henrietta Wirt. His father was a Swiss, his
mother a German ; the first died when he was
yet an infant, the latter when he was but eight
years old. An orphan at this tender age, he
passed into the family and guardianship of his
uncle, Jasper Wirt, who, as well as his wife, was
a Swiss by birth, and then resided near the same

village, not far, we think, from the Washington
road.   Mr. Wirt retains very vivid impressions
of the character of his aunt, which are worth
preserving, both as an amiable picture of a pious
and constant temper, and as an evidence of early
observation in the relater.   He has always spoken
of her as having a cast of character worthy of
the land of William Tell.   She was tall and
rather large framed, with a fair complexion, and
a face that must have been handsome in youth.
Her kindliness of temper seems to have made its
usual indelible impression on sensitive and lively
childhood, whose little errors often require that
tender disposition to excuse, which is sure to be
repaid by its warm gratitude.   With this allow-
ance for the weakness of others, she seems to
have had none of her own, possessing a fine
mind, and an uncommon mixture of firmness
and sensibility.   She was very religious, and
a great reader of pious books, of which one, an
old folio German Bible or family expositor, in
its binding of wood or black leather, with brass
clasps, was held in venerable remembrance by
the boy, struck, no doubt, by the air and voice
of devotion and deep feeling with which she was
accustomed to read the consolatory volume aloud.
A little incident exhibits a touch of heroism in

her not unworthy to be related. A thunderstorm came up one evening unusually violent, and as the lightning became more terrific, the aunt got down her Bible, and began to read aloud. The women were exceedingly frightened, especially when one appalling flash struck a tree in the yard, and drove a large splinter towards them. They flew from their chairs into the darkest corners of the room. The aunt alone remained firm in her seat, at a table in the middle of the floor, and noticed the peal in no other way than by the increased energy of her voice. This contrast struck the young observer, then not more than six years of age, with so much force, that he describes the scene as fresh before him to the present moment, and as giving him an early impression of the superiour dignity with which firmness and piety invest the character.

Most lively boys remember pretty faithfully the picturesque scenes or incidents of their childhood, the village green, the haunted house, the first advent of the rope-dancer, and those " Circensian games" with which they are as universally captivated as were the Roman People themselves. The personages also that figured in the early scene, are remembered with some general notion of their being venerable or ridicu-

lous, good-natured or cross, in the reputation of
the neighbourhood, or in the apprehension of the
urchin himself. Our future jurisprudent might
be thought to be born for a painter or a dramatist, to judge from his oddly minute memory of
localities, persons and costume. The village of
Bladensburg was at this time the most active
and bustling place of trade in Maryland. It
stands in the midst of a tobacco country, and
was then the great place of export for the state.
There was a large "tobacco inspection" there,
several rich resident merchants, and some Scotch
and other foreign factors, with large capitals.
During this its "high and palmy state," a lot in
it was worth the price of three of the best lots in
Georgetown, Belhaven, (now Alexandria,) or
Baltimore. It is now a decayed, ruinous ham-
let, through which the late Attorney-General of
the United States has often passed, in his professional journeys, with those natural emotions, no
doubt, which such a spot, revisited under such
circumstances, might excite in minds of less
poetical sensibility than his. But if there is a
complacent satisfaction to be envied on earth, it
is that which must often have arisen in his mind
in retracing this scene of his childhood. At that
day the free empire in which he was to be an

ornament and a conspicuous actor, had not even
an existence; and little did those foresee, who
caressed him as an apt, imitative boy, that on
hills almost within sight of his humble patrimo-
nial roof, proud domes were to arise in which he
was to discharge the functions of the highest
legal office of the republic, and sit in council on
its most momentous concerns. When a few
years afterward it was a question with his guar-
'dian whether to continue his education with the
small means devolved from his father, an expression was let fall by his worthy and not undis-
cerning aunt, involuntarily prophetic. In urging
that he should be continued at school, "When
I look at that dear child," said she, " he hardly
seems one of us, and I weep when I think of
him." They were doubtless tears of joyful pride,
the full measure of which it is as natural and
frequent a wish, as it is often a vain one, that
the tender guardians of youthful promise might
oftener live to feel.

In his seventh year he was sent from home
to school; a melancholy era in the memory of
most boys. There was a classical school in
Georgetown, eight miles from Bladensburg, under the direction of a Mr. Rogers, and the boy
was placed to board at the house of a Quaker of

the name of Scholfield, who occupied a small log
house on Bridge-street. His wife was a kind
creature, whose good nature was touched by the
grief of the child at his first exile from home,
and displayed itself in many characteristic topics
of consolation, remembered to this day by a temper naturally sensitive and grateful. Among
other little expedients by which the good-natured
woman sought to allay the burst of boyish sorrow, she had recourse to the story of Joseph in
Egypt. She made him enter into the distresses
of the son and his aged father in their separation,
and so forget his own; insinuating that, as the
separation had brought Joseph to great honours,
so his might turn out equally fortunate.

When the boy grew to be a man, he went to
see kind Mrs. Scholfield, and a warmer meeting
seldom takes place between mother and son.
Schools for teaching the classics were rare in
those days, and Mr. Rogers's contained quite a
small army of boys and young men, of whom
Richard Brent, since a member of Congress
from Virginia, was one. Our tyro remained at
it less than a year, and never had much pleasure
in recollecting it, perhaps from some injudicious
rigour, which he thought had the effect of breaking his spirit. He was transferred to a classical

school in Charles county, Maryland, about forty miles from Bladensburg, and boarded with an old widow lady of the name of Love. The school was kept by one Hatch Dent, in the vestry-house of Newport church. Here, being a lively boy, he was a great favourite in the family, and seems to have been as happy as a boy can be, separated from the natural objects of his affection, and with nothing to mar his pleasure except going to school and getting tasks in the holydays, the latter of which seems to have been an ingenious contrivance of our forefathers to deform the elysium of vacations by an early hint of the transitoriness of pleasure. In these changes from place to place, he appears to have been fortunate in finding kind friends; a circumstance which, as it arose out of a natural goodness of disposition, accompanied him through life.

Mr. Dent was a most excellent man, very good-tempered, who either found no occasion, or, with the exception of a single application of the ferrule, no inclination, to punish his young pupil, who in two years advanced as far as Cæsar's Commentaries, though perhaps without being properly grounded in his author. Here, as at Georgetown, there was quite a crowd of boys, and several young men fully grown.

Among the latter was Alexander Campbell, who afterward became well known in Virginia as an orator, and still more for his untimely and melancholy death. This accomplished and unfortunate gentleman, of whose argument in the case of Ray and Garnett, reported in Washington's Reports, Mr. Pendleton, the President of the Court of Appeals, is said to have spoken as the most perfect model of forensic discussion he had ever heard, was then from eighteen to twenty years of age, manly and dignified in his deportment, and of a grave and thoughtful air, occasionally, only, relaxed into a gayer mood, and with that remarkable tremulous eye by which others of his family were also distinguished. He had just gained the prize of eloquence in the school at Georgetown, and his manners perhaps as much as his age procured him from the school-boys at Mr. Dent's, the title of *Mr.* Campbell. He began his career at the bar some years after Chief Justice Marshall and Judge Washington, who must themselves have commenced practice after the Revolutionary War. Edmund Randolph began a little before, or perhaps just at the breaking out of the war, and Patrick Henry about fifteen years earlier. All these celebrated men were still at the bar when

Mr. Campbell appeared at it; he was engaged frequently in the same causes with them, and it is a high praise to say that even among them he was a distinguished man. Mr. Wirt has said of him, "he did not wield the Herculean club of Marshall, nor did his rhetoric exhibit the Gothic magnificence of Henry; but his quiver was furnished with arrows polished to the finest point, that were launched with Apollonian skill and grace." He was yet at the bar of the superiour courts of Virginia, when Mr. Wirt had grown up and commenced the practice of law in the upper part of that state, and was held to stand in the first rank of genius. The latter adds, "Some of the most beautiful touches of eloquence I have ever heard, were echoes from Campbell which reached us in our mountains." This promising career was cut short by a lamentable death. He left a whimsical will, in which, among other odd things, was a request that no stone might be laid on his grave, for the reason that, if a stone were placed on every grave, there would be no earth left for tillage.

From Mr. Dent's, the subject of our memoir was removed in his eleventh year, to a very flourishing school kept by the Rev. James Hunt, a Presbyterian clergyman in Montgomery county,

Maryland. At this school he remained till it
was broken up, that is, till 1787, and here, during a period of four years, he received the principal part of his education, being carried through
all the Latin and Greek classics then usually
taught in grammar-schools, and instructed in
geography and some of the branches of the
mathematics, including arithmetic, trigonometry,
surveying, and the first six books of Euclid's
Elements. During the last two years of the
time, he boarded with Mr. Hunt. This gentleman was a graduate of Princeton college, of
some learning, fond of conversation and reading,
and when engaged in the latter, of evenings,
would sometimes read to the boys any interesting
passages of the book before him. One of his
favourites was Josephus, in which our youth
was as much taken with the account of the historian's defence of the fortified town of Jotapata,
as Kotzebue tells us he was captivated in like
manner by the story of the siege of Jerusalem.
Our clergyman, who in his suit of black velvet
was quite a stately and graceful person, had a
pair of globes and a telescope, with the aid of
which, and by conversation, he gave his pupils
some smattering of astronomy. Added to these
was an electrical machine, with which he took

pleasure in making experiments, to the entertainment and instruction not only of his scholars,
but of the ladies and gentlemen of the neighbourhood. But the most important part of his pos-
sessions was a good general library, in which
our youth, now a lad of twelve or thirteen, first
contracted a passion for reading, or fed it rather,
it being first kindled by " Guy, Earl of War-
wick," which he obtained from a carpenter in the
employ of Mr. Hunt, and further fanned by a
fragment of Peregrine Pickle, neither of which
famous works, probably, was found in the library
of the reverend preceptor. Those which made
the nearest approach to them were the British
Dramatists, which our reader devoured with
insatiable appetite, and, having exhausted them,
was driven from necessity on the works of Pope
and Addison, and then on Horne's Elements of
Criticism. As this reading was wholly a voluntary, and somewhat furtive affair on his part, he
drifted along through the library pretty much
like the hero of Waverley and the historian of
Waverley himself, as chance or caprice directed,
mastering nothing perhaps, yet increasing his
stock of ideas, and deriving some cultivation of
taste from the exercise; a sort of reading much
too captivating and absorbing to the youthful

mind not to impregnate it with thought, and fit
it, at all events, for better directed efforts; as the
shedding from our forests prepares a richer soil
for the hand of regular cultivation. The discovery that Pope began to compose at twelve
years of age, begat in our student the same sort
of emulation as the like example in Cowley did
in Pope. He reproached himself for his back-
wardness when he was now already thirteen.
The first attempt was a little discouraging. It
was in verse, and he was embarrassed as usual
by the awkward alternative of sacrificing the
rhythm to the thought, or (which is the usual
preference in such cases,) the thought to the
rhythm. He came to the disappointing conclusion that he was no poet, but indemnified himself by more lucky efforts in prose, one of which
falling into the hands of Mr. Hunt, he expressed
his favourable surprise, and exhorted the adventurer to persevere, who thus encouraged became
a confirmed reader and author.

One of these juvenile essays was engendered
by a school incident, and was a piece of revenge,
more legitimate than schoolboy invention is apt
to inflict when sharpened by wrongs real or
imaginary. There was an usher at the school,
and this usher, who was more learned and me-

thodical than even-tempered, was one morning
delayed in the customary routine by the absence
of his principal scholar, who was young Wirt
himself. In his impatience he went often to the
door, and espying some boys clinging like a
knot of bees to a cherry-tree not far off, he con-
cluded that the expected absentee was of the
number, and nursed his wrath accordingly.
The truth was, that the servant of a neighbour
with whom Wirt was boarded at the time, had
gone that morning to mill, and the indispensable
breakfast had been delayed by his late return.
This apology, however, was urged in vain on
the usher, who charged in corroboration the
plunder of the cherry-tree; and though this was
as stoutly as truly rejoined to be the act of an
English school hard by, the recitation of master Wirt proceeded under very threatening prog-
nostics of storm. The lesson was in Cicero,
and at every hesitation of the reciter, the eloquent volume, brandished by the yet chafing
tutor, descended within an inch of his head,
without quailing his facetiousness however, for
he said archly, "take care, or you'll kill me."
We have heard better timed jests since from the
dexterous orator, for the next slip brought a blow
in good earnest, which being as forcible as if

Logic herself, with her "closed fist," had dealt it, felled our hero to the ground. "I'll pay you for this, if I live," said the fallen champion, as he rose from the field. "Pay me, will you?" said the usher, quite furious; "you will never live to do that." "Yes, I will," said the boy.

Our youth was an author, be it remembered, and that is not a race to take an injury, much less an affront, calmly. The quill, too, was a fair weapon against an usher, and by way of vent to his indignation at this and other continued outrages, but with no view to what so seriously fell out from it in furtherance of his revenge, he indited some time afterward an ethical essay on Anger. In this, after due exhibition of its unhappy effects, which, it may be, would have enlightened Seneca, though he has himself professed to treat the same subject, he reviewed those relations and functions of life most exposed to the assaults of this Fury. A parent with an undutiful son, said our moralist, must often be very angry;—a master with his servant, an inn-keeper with his guests;—but it is an usher that must the oftenest be vexed by this bad passion, and, right or wrong, find himself in a terrible rage; and so he went on, in a manner very edifying, and very descriptive of

the case, character and manner of the expounder
of Cicero. Well pleased with his work, our
author found a most admiring reader in an elder
boy, who, charmed with the mischief as much
as the wit of the occasion, pronounced it a most
excellent performance, and very fit for a Satur-
day morning's declamation. In vain did our
wit object strenuously the dangers of this mode
of publication. The essay was "got by heart,"
and declaimed in the presence of the school and
of the usher himself, who, enraged at the satire,
demanded the writer, otherwise threatening the
declaimer with the rod. His magnanimity was
not proof against this, and he betrayed the
incognito of our author, who happened the same
evening to be in his garret when master usher,
the obnoxious satire in hand, came into the
apartment below to lay his complaint before his
principal. Mr. Hunt's house was one of those
one-story rustic mansions yet to be seen in Maryland, where the floor of the attic, without the
intervention of ceiling, forms the roof of the
apartment below, so that the culprit could easily
be the hearer, and even the partial spectator, of
the inquisition held on his case. "Let us see
this offensive libel," said the preceptor, and awful
were the first silent moments of its perusal,

which were broken, first by a suppressed titter,
and finally, to the mighty relief of the listener,
by a loud burst of laughter. "Pooh! pooh!
Mr. ——, this is but the sally of a lively boy,
and best say no more about it; besides that, *in
foro conscientiæ*, we can hardly find him guilty
of the 'publication.'" This was a victory; and
when Mr. Hunt left the room, the conqueror,
tempted to sing his "Io triumphe" in some song
allusive to the country of the discomfited party,
who was a foreigner, was put to flight by the
latter's rushing furiously into the attic, and
snatching from under his pillow some hickories,
the fasces of his office, and inflicting some smart
strokes on the flying satirist, who did not stay,
like Voltaire, to write a receipt for them. The
usher left the school in dudgeon not long afterward, like the worthy in the doggerel rhymes, —

> " The hero who did 'sist upon't
> He wouldn't be deputy to Mr. Hunt."

Many years after, the usher and his scholar
met again. Age and poverty had overtaken the
poor man, and his former pupil had the opportunity of showing him some kindnesses which
were probably not lessened by the recollection of
this unpremeditated revenge.

Another little incident that occurred at this

school had some effect in shaping the fortunes of the subject of this sketch. Mr. Hunt was in the habit of giving his boys one day in the court week at Montgomery court-house, to go and hear the lawyers plead. There were then some distinguished men at that bar, and among them one who had just commenced practice, the late William H. Dorsey. This was a great treat to the boys, who made their way on foot, early of a morning, to the court-house, about four miles; took their position in some gallery or box, from which they could hear and see all that passed; and looked and listened with all the greedy attention of young rustics at their first visit to a theatre. The struggles of young Dorsey with the veterans opposed to him, found most favour in the eyes of these exoterick disciples of the law. He was fluent, keen, animated and dexterous, and as often the foiler as the foiled. This sport was so delightful to them that they determined to have a court of their own, and Wirt was appointed to draft a constitution and body of laws, which he reported accordingly, with an apologetic letter prefixed. In this court he was a practitioner of eminence. The semi-annual examinations and exhibitions at the school afforded another theatre of competition. On these occasions they delivered speeches and acted plays, and as Mr. Hunt had high notions of oratory, and duly instructed them in tone and gesture, and as there were always large audiences of gentlemen and ladies, the occasion was full of excitement and emulation. Wirt bore off one of the prizes of eloquence at these exhibitions ; his speech was a prologue of Farquhar's, adapted to the occasion by Mr. Hunt, and, young as he was, he could not help suspecting that his reverend teacher's partiality for his own work had some share in the award of the preference. There was another exercise at this school, now, we believe, fallen into disuse, at least in America. This was " capping verses," as it is called,—a sort of game of the memory to which we suspect the orators of St. Stephen's chapel are as much indebted for the quotations from the classics in vogue there, as to any warm poetic sensibility. In this exercise, which is not an unuseful one, the boys became at length so well supplied with the appropriate weapons, that the venerable teacher had to close it himself, which he was wont to do with Virgil's "Claudite jam rivos, pueri, sat prata biberunt."

When Mr. Hunt's school was broken up, his pupil was but fifteen, and his little patrimony being insufficient either to support him at college or meet the expense of a professional education he was exposed to the danger of an idle residence in the village of Bladensburg, under no other control than that which his guardian thought proper to exercise, which practically was no control at all. From the dangers of this situation the "constitution" and prefatory letter before mentioned, chanced to be instrumental in delivering him. Among the boys at school when that juvenile trifle was produced, was Ninian Edwards, the late governor of Illinois, the son of Mr. Benjamin Edwards, who resided in Montgomery county, and subsequently represented that district in Congress. On his return home, young Edwards took with him the aforesaid constitution and letter for the amusement of his father; and that gentleman fancied that he saw something of promise in the letter which deserved a better fate than the young author's seemed likely to be. On the evidence of this little essay, for he had never seen him, and learning that he had completed the course of the grammar-school, and had not the means to push his education further; perhaps, too, on the favourable report of his school-fellows, he kindly wrote to invite him to take up his residence in

his family, where, he said, he could prepare the
writer's son and nephews for college, while he
could at the same time continue his studies with
the aid of the small library there. The invita-
tion was accepted, and fortunately so, it being
Mr. Wirt's conviction, often expressed, that it
was to this gentleman's peculiar and happy cast
of character that he owed most of what may be
praiseworthy in his own. Mr. Edwards's education was limited; but he had that natural vigour
of mind which more than atones for its defects.
He had found leisure, nevertheless, amidst his
occupations as planter and merchant, to acquaint
himself with the historians, from whom he had
imbibed as lively a veneration for the Catos
and Brutuses as Algernon Sydney himself.
His own person and presence had much of the
heroic character. To these he added a polite
and easy manner, which, though a little stately
abroad, was sportive and facetious in private.
This gentleman, so well adapted to win the
regard of a young man, while his character presented a model very proper to be imitated, was
also a natural orator, unaffected, but with all
that unction which natural benignity imparts.
On some occasion that concerned the interests of
his country, he pronounced a maiden speech in

the assembly of Maryland, which was so well
received by the patriot, Samuel Chase, that he
came across the house, and warmly congratula-
ted the speaker.   He had a melodious and flexi-
ble voice, his enunciation was distinct and clear,
and his language astonishingly copious, correct
and appropriate.   A still better point than these
for forming a young mind, was the candour and
moderation of his way of thinking.   Intellectual
arrogance, he often took occasion to say, was the
strongest proof of ignorance and imbecility; and
though an independent thinker, with bold and
original conceptions, he liked to draw out those
about him to combat his opinions.   One dwells
with satisfaction on characters of this cast, of
which our revolutionary age, like all other great
and stirring crises, was profuse.   Indeed, Mr.
Edwards added to the properties we have described, the full inspiration of that remarkable
period ; and having been conversant with its
scenes and its actors, felt that warm and high
patriotism which the difficulties and the happy
issue of the struggle were equally adapted to
create.

This kind and judicious man, whose share in
forming the character of his young friend, and
giving his fortunes a favourable turn, has led us

to speak of him more at large, took great pains
to draw out the qualities and talents of the youth
from the cloud of a natural bashfulness. This
timidity was so great that he could scarcely get
through a sentence intelligibly; and to correct
this bias of temper, his friend endeavoured to
raise his estimate of himself, kindly reminding
him of his natural advantages, and that, in the
common phrase, the game of his fortune was in
his own hand. He pointed his attention to
many men who had emerged from an obscure
condition by force of their own exertions; efforts
to which our political institutions were especially
propitious, as they threw open the lists of honour
to generous emulation. " Mr. Dorsey," said he,
"whom you so much admire, and Mr. Pinkney,
whom you have not seen, but who is more worthy still of your admiration, are making their
own way to distinction, under as great disadvan-
tages as any you have to encounter." These
encouragements and assurances were regarded
bv the youth as kindly overcharging his advi-
.er's real estimate of him, and as a kind of pious
fraud, intended for his good; till many years
after, when he was chancellor at Williamsburg,
in Virginia, he received a long letter from his old
friend, reminding him of these predictions, and

adding that he considered his career as only
begun.

Mr. Wirt's enunciation was at this time of
life thick and hasty, and he was alternately
counselled and rallied on this defect by his
friend, whose discernment and native goodness
of heart, seem equally to have engaged him in
developing the mind and manners of the young
man, and urging him upon a career befitting his
natural good parts.   As this impeded utterance
arose chiefly from the bashfulness which Mr.
Edwards, as we have said, took such kind
means to counteract, the latter, among other examples of encouragement, used to tell the story
of his own *debut* in the Maryland Assembly,
when, as he declared, his alarm spread such a
mist before his eyes that he spoke, as it were, in
the dark, and was surprised to find from Mr.
Chase's congratulation, that he had even been
talking sense.   He at the same time directed
our youth's attention to historical studies, which
had formed no part of his reading in his miscellaneous and accidental selections from Mr.
Hunt's library.

Under the roof of Mr. Edwards, or in his
immediate neighbourhood, the subject of our
memoir remained about twenty months, in the

occupations already described. These increased his familiarity with the Latin and Greek classics, and led him to exercises of his own pen, which often served for the declamations of the boys under his instruction. Thus, at a most critical age, and under circumstances which but for Mr. Edwards, might have plunged him into that idle career which is often the consequence of discouraging prospects, he was engaged in a course of life highly favourable to his mental habits, while in the lessons and example of a valuable friend, he found not less propitious impulses to his morals, and to raising his hopes and views in life. It were ascribing too much sway to mere accident in " shaping our ends," not to interpose a remark which these anecdotes may have already suggested. Doubtless the merit was not small which could awake so friendly and tender a concern ; and must, under any circumstances, have attracted regard, and found efficient friends. Men seldom achieve more than they deserve ; a proposition for the most part denied by those only who in some way have been wanting to themselves.

In this year, 1789, showing some symptoms of what was feared to be consumption, he was advised, by his physician, to pass the winter in

a southern climate. He went accordingly on
horseback, as far as Augusta, in Georgia, and
remained there till the following spring. On his
return, he commenced the study of law at Montgomery court-house, with Mr. William P. Hunt,
the son of his old preceptor; this he pursued
subsequently with Mr. Thomas Swann, now the
United States' Attorney for the District of Co-
lumbia, on whose application, aided by his good
offices, he obtained a license for practice in the
autumn of 1792. In the same autumn he removed to Culpepper court-house, in Virginia,
and commenced his professional career there,
being at the time only twenty years of age.

His health had now become confirmed, and
he entered with the advantage of a vigorous
constitution, on a profession whose toilsomeness
renders that advantage hardly less essential to
splendid success, than, in the opinion of the
Great Captain of the age, it was to military fortune. He had, from nature, the further recom-
mendation of a good person and carriage, and
of a prepossessing appearance. The urbanity
which now belongs to him, was then alloyed by
some impetuousness of manner. It arose, we
believe, chiefly out of his own diffidence, a feeling which often makes the expression turbid,

and gives an air of vehemence to what is only
hurry. His utterance was still faulty. A friend
who knew him a little after this period says, that
when heated by argument, his ideas seemed to
outstrip his power of expression; his tongue
appeared too large; he clipped some of his
words sadly; his voice, sweet and musical in
conversation, grew loud and harsh, his articula-
tion rapid, indistinct and imperfect. With these
advantages and defects, such as they were, he
was to begin the competitions of the bar in a part
of the country where he was quite unknown, and
where much talent had preoccupied the ground
with experience on its side, and acquaintance
with the people and their affairs. There is no
part of the world where, more than in Virginia,
these embarrassments would be lessened to a
new adventurer; as there is nowhere a more
courteous race of gentlemen, accessible to the
prepossessions which merit excites. There was
however another embarrassment; our lawyer
had no cause; but he encountered here a young
friend much in the same circumstances, but
who had a single case, which he proposed to
share with Wirt as the means of making a joint
debut; and with this small stock in trade, they
went to attend the first county-court.

Their case was one of joint assault and battery, with joint judgment against three, of whom
two had been released subsequently to the judgment, and the third, who had been taken in
execution, and imprisoned, claimed the benefit
of that release as enuring to himself. Under
these circumstances, the matter of discharge
having happened since the judgment, the old
remedy was by the writ of *audita querela*. But
Mr. Wirt and his associate had learned from
their Blackstone that the indulgence of courts in
modern times, in granting summary relief, in
such cases, by motion, had, in a great measure,
superseded the use of the old writ; and accordingly presented their case in the form of a motion.

The motion was opened by Wirt's friend, with
all the alarm of a first essay. The bench was
then, in Virginia county-courts, composed of the
ordinary justices of the peace; and the elder
members of the bar, by a usage the more necessary from the constitution of the tribunal, frequently interposed as *amici curiæ*, or informers
of the conscience of the court. It appears that
on the case being opened, some of these customary advisers denied that a release to one after
judgment released the other, and they denied also

the propriety of the form of proceeding. The
ire of our beginner was kindled by this reception
of his friend, and by this voluntary interference
with their motion; and, when he came to reply,
he forgot the natural alarms of the occasion, and
maintained his point with recollection and firmness. This awaked the generosity of an elder
member of the bar, a person of consideration in
the neighbourhood, and a good lawyer. He
stepped in as an auxiliary, remarking that he
also was *amicus curiæ*, and perhaps as much
entitled to act as such, as others; in which capacity he would state his conviction of the propriety of the motion, and that the court was not
at liberty to disregard it; adding that its having
come from a new quarter gave it but a stronger
claim on the candour and urbanity of a Virginian
bar. The two friends carried their point in
triumph, and the worthy ally told his brethren,
in his plain phrase, that they had best make fair
weather with one who promised to be "a thorn
in their side." The advice was, we dare say,
unnecessary. The bar of that county wanted
neither talent nor courtesy; and the champion
having vindicated his pretensions to enter the
lists, was thenceforward engaged in many a
courteous "passage at arms."

The auxiliary mentioned in the above anecdote was the late General John Miner, of Fredericksburg, of whom Mr. Wirt, in subsequent years, often spoke with strong gratitude and esteem. " There was never," he says, " a more finished and engaging gentleman, nor one of a more warm, honest, and affectionate heart. He was as brave a man, and as true a patriot, as ever lived. He was a most excellent lawyer too, with a most persuasive flow of eloquence, simple natural, graceful, and most affecting wherever there was room for pathos ; and his pathos was not artificial rhetoric ; it was of that true sort which flows from a feeling heart, and a noble mind. He was my firm and constant friend from that day through a long life ; and took occasion, several times in after years, to remind me of his prophecy, and to insist on my obligation to sustain his ' prophetic reputation.' He left a large and most respectable family, and lives embalmed in the hearts of all who knew him."

In a year or two he extended his practice to the neighbouring county of Albemarle, where, in the spring of 1795, he married Mildred, the eldest daughter of Doctor George Gilmer, and took up his residence at Pen Park, the seat of

that gentleman, near Charlottesville. The family
with which he formed this connexion, was in
the first rank of society, a condition which it
adorned with substantial excellence, with the
graces that give elegance to life, and with a full
share of Virginian hospitality. His father-in-
law was among the most eminent physicians of
the day, but not more distinguished for professional skill than for his classical learning and
his eloquence; and he is well remembered in
Virginia for a flow of pure, natural wit; to
which he added the higher charm of warm benevolence. Of these qualities his daughter in-
herited a large portion, and was a woman of
rare endowments both of mind and heart. The
removal of Mr. Wirt brought him into a very
agreeable and desirable neighbourhood, and introduced him to the acquaintance of many persons of much worth, some of them of high
celebrity, among whom it is sufficient to mention Mr. Monroe and Mr. Jefferson, whose cordial
friendship he gained and held without abatement
to the end of their lives. Dr. Gilmer was the
intimate friend and constant associate of both
these gentlemen, as well as of Mr. Madison, who
lived in the next county, and was in the habit
of visiting Monticello and its neighbourhood; and

he thus brought his son-in-law into an intercourse with these eminent men.   Mr. Wirt's
serious associations in life have been of this uniform stamp.   "Doctores sapientiæ secutus est,
qui sola bona quæ honesta, mala tantum quæ
turpia." It was here, in the latter part of 1796,
that the gentleman to whose sketch we have
mentioned ourselves to be indebted, first saw
and made acquaintance with him.   He had
never, he says, met with any man so highly
engaging and prepossessing.   His figure was
strikingly elegant and commanding, with a face
of the first order of masculine beauty, animated,
and expressing high intellect.   His manners
took the tone of his heart; they were frank,
open and cordial; and his conversation, to which
his reading and early pursuits had given a classic tinge, was very polished, gay and witty.
Altogether, his friend adds, he was a most fasci-
nating companion, and to those of his own age
irresistibly and universally winning.   This was
a dangerous eminence to one of his social turn
and mercurial temperament, as the young and
gay sought his company with eagerness.   The
intellectual bias, however, was that which prevailed, and filled his hours of retirement with
befitting studies.   He read and wrote constantly

and habitually, earnestly employing the periods
thus "dedicate to closeness and the bettering of his
mind," in studying the fathers of English literature, Bacon, Boyle, Locke, Hooker and others, with
whose works the excellent library of Dr. Gilmer
abounded. In this course of study and social
enjoyment interchanged, his mind improved by
habitual intercourse with men who were already
the personages of history, he continued to reside
at Pen Park, practising professionally in the surrounding counties.

His business was rapidly increasing, and he
was already considered as well one of the best
lawyers in the circle of his practice, as destined
to greater eminence, when, in September, 1799,
he lost his wife, to whom he was tenderly attached, and with whom he had lived most happily.
Their union was not blessed with children.
This event fell heavily on his spirits, and broke
in, for a time, on his professional occupations
and aims; and with a view, we believe, to
diverting his chagrin by change of scene, his
friends urged him to allow himself to be nomi
nated in the next election of Clerk of the House
of Delegates. This was pressed also by several
members of influence in the House. He con-
sented, and was elected. The duties of this

office occupied only a few of the winter months. A respectable salary was attached to it, and it had been held by several persons of character and celebrity,—by John Randolph, by his son Edmund, and by Wythe, the venerable Chancellor of Virginia. It brought him into familiar intercourse with another circle of the active and vigorous minds of the state, among them many choice, gay spirits, to whom the wit and other fascinations of the new clerk carried their usual allurement. His immediate predecessor, John Stewart, of witty memory, had been displaced from political considerations, the republican party having just gained the ascendency. It was a period of great political excitement in Virginia. The celebrated "Resolutions of 1798" in relation to the Alien and Sedition laws, had been passed in the Assembly the preceding year, and the ensuing session of the legislature was expected with unusual interest by both the parties into which the fundamental constitutional questions that had by that time taken body and shape, had divided not the state only, but the whole Union. The illustrious Patrick Henry, who in this question took side with the general government, had been elected to the House of Delegates, and suitable preparation was made to oppose in that

assembly an adversary who, though infirm with
age and disease, was still regarded as formidable.
Mr. Madison, Mr. Giles, Mr. Taylor of Carolina,
and Mr. Nicholas, were arrayed against the vete-
ran, who never came, however, to the conflict.
His death, which happened not long before the
session of the Assembly, disappointed Mr. Wirt
of seeing the subject of his future biography, and
left him to paint the picture from tradition, to
which his actual contemplation of the man
might have given its most characteristic touches.

He held the post of Clerk, by two succeeding
elections, till February, 1802.   In the mean-
time he did not wholly relinquish his practice,
and volunteered, in 1800, as counsel for the
accused in the trial of Callender, whose prosecution makes such a figure in the domestic political
history of the United States.   Mr. Wirt, it may
be remembered from a popular anecdote, did not
escape his share of the judicial asperities which
gave such offence to Callender's counsel, and
afterward made part of the charges in the im-
peachment of the judge.   The latter appears to
have appreciated his equableness of temper and
manners.   During the trial or shortly after it,
meeting the father of Mr. Wirt's second wife, he
asked after his son-in-law with some marks of

regard. "They did not summon *him*," he observed, "on my trial; had I known it, I might have summoned him myself; yet it was only to that young man I said any thing exceptionable, or which I have thought of with regret since." On the fourth of July, 1800, Mr. Wirt was selected by the democratic party at Richmond, to pronounce the anniversary oration. This brief composition, which we have seen, is fervid and rapid, and has so unpremeditated an air, and was pronounced, we have heard, so little like other prepared orations, as to have been thought extemporary.

In 1802 the legislature of Virginia gave him an unexpected proof of its confidence and esteem. It was found necessary at this time to divide the business of the court of Chancery, in which Mr. Wythe then presided, a man of the deepest learning, and the best civilian that ever appeared in that state. Of three chancery districts now created, Mr. Wirt was appointed Chancellor of the eastern, comprehending the Eastern Shore of Virginia, and all the counties below Richmond. This appointment was wholly unexpected to him till the very moment before the election came on in the House of Delegates, and his first notice of it, we believe, was his being requested by his friends to withdraw till the nomination should be made, and the votes taken. Sensible of the gravity of the trust, he went, even after the election, to Mr. Monroe, then governor of Virginia, to express an apprehension of its unsuitableness to either his years or attainments. Mr. Monroe replied that the legislature, he doubted not, knew very well what it was doing, and that it was not probable he would disappoint either it or the suitors in the court. Mr. Wirt was then but twenty-nine years of age, and his appointment to a court whose jurisdiction involves important interests, and requires weight of character, and integrity, as much as extensive attainments, was an emphatic mark of consideration from men who, from his post of Clerk to the House, had opportunities of knowing him more than usually familiar. The duties of the chancellorship called him to reside at Williamsburg, where he presided in his court with industry and ability, and with equal satisfaction to counsel and parties. In the autumn of the same year he married Elizabeth, a daughter of the late Colonel Gamble, of Richmond; an estimable lady, still living, in the bosom of a large family of sons and daughters.

This marriage led to his resignation of the

chancellorship, and his resumption of the practice of law. The salary was inadequate to support a family; but other considerations probably
conduced to this step. Emulation is not extinct
at thirty, and a more stirring scene of action was
perhaps more agreeable to his temperament. In
the first instance he designed a removal to Kentucky, and had even made some preparations
with that view. But Mr. Tazewell, who then
resided at Norfolk, earnestly urged him on the
contrary to remove thither, and enforced his
advice with many friendly representations and
offers. We believe it was chiefly owing to the
influence of this gentleman, then already eminent in the profession which he adorns, that Mr.
Wirt abandoned his design of going to the west,
and went, in the winter of 1803—4, to reside at
Norfolk.

Just after his resigning the chancellorship, he
was employed, together with Mr. Tazewell and
Mr. Semple, afterward Judge Semple, in the
defence of a man apprehended and tried on some
points of circumstantial evidence so curious, that
we are tempted to relate them. A person named
St. George, who resided near Williamsburg, was
shot dead one night through the window of his
own house. No trace appeared of the assassin,

nor any circumstances that could indicate his
enemy; only some duck-shot appeared in the
wall, near the ceiling. While the crowd called
out by the scene, stood confounded around the
dead body, a bystander, who had been employed
by the late Chancellor, a person remarkable to
some degree of oddity for his habits of close and
curious investigation, went out of the house, and
placing himself in the line of direction that the
shot must have taken to the spot where they
lodged, endeavoured to ascertain from that circumstance the exact position of the person
who discharged the gun. While thus occupied,
his eye was caught by a very small piece of
paper on the ground betwixt himself and the
window, which appeared, on taking up, to have
been part of the wadding, and had on it what
seemed to be two of the three strokes composing
the letter *m*. One of the crowd exclaimed at
this moment, "I wonder where Shannon is;
has any one seen Shannon?" Shannon was
the son-in-law of the deceased, and resided on
the opposite shore of the James river; and it
was soon ascertained that he had been seen in
Williamsburg that day, with a gun on his shoul-
der. The gun, however, had no cock upon it,
and a blacksmith to whom he had gone to have it

repaired, stated that Shannon had left his work-shop with it in this condition. The man was pursued, nevertheless, over the river, and to his own house, to which he was found not to have returned; and was traced at length to a tavern, some thirty miles off, and caught in bed with all his clothes on, sound asleep. He was seized as he lay, and on being searched, some duck shot was found about him, and a letter, with part of it torn off. When this letter was afterward compared with the fragment of the wadding, the two were found to fit, and the letter *m*, before mentioned, to form part of the word *my* in the letter. On these circumstances, strengthened by the fact that the death of his father-in-law would have put Shannon in possession of his wife's fortune, he was brought to trial. A single juryman "stood out," as the phrase is, for ten days, and the defendant was discharged in consequence of this disagreement among his triers. No other circumstances ever threw light on the truth of this transaction. Some person, struck with Mr. Wirt's defence in the case, and having a remarkable memory, afterward repeated it with little variation.

It was immediately before his removal to Norfolk that Mr. Wirt wrote the letters published in the Richmond Argus under the title of " The British Spy," which form part of the present volume. They were composed in a great degree for diversion of mind, with little care, and with still less expectation of the favourable reception they met at the time, or of the popularity they retained afterward. They have since been collected into a small volume, of which the present is the tenth edition. The sketches of living characters were received with a good deal of curiosity by the public, and are probably faithful pictures.

At Norfolk he found for competitors the Tazewells, the Taylors, the Neversons and others, men in the first rank of their profession, who at that time adorned its bar. In a commercial place too, whose foreign commerce was then very extensive, the questions most abundant before the courts were those of maritime law, to which in the theatre of his former practice he had been wholly a stranger, but to which he now applied himself with that indefatigable labour of which few men are more capable. There are no more willing witnesses than his opponents, of his learning, and vigorous conduct of his causes, and, consequently, his rapid rise in the public esteem. He continued to practise in Norfolk

and in the courts of the surrounding counties till
1806, when he once more changed his residence
to Richmond, solicited to it by his family and
friends, who conceived that he would find there
a wider and more lucrative professional field.
In this city he remained till his appointment to
the Attorney-Generalship of the United States.

Among the names which then gave remarkable celebrity to the Richmond bar, were those
of Edmund Randolph, John Wickham, Daniel
Call, George Hay, and George Keith Taylor,
not to mention several others who mingled their
rays in what was quite a constellation of legal
learning and talents. If the competitions of
such a theatre required all his resources, they
were also of a nature to fashion and strengthen
them. The sphere of his business and his reputation enlarged according to the expectation of
his friends. He was often called into distant
parts of the country both in criminal and great
civil causes, and in the course of a various practice of more than ten years, with men of abilities
as various, he rose in the general opinion to a
level with the first of them. He seems at no
point of his career, nor in any of the different
scenes to which it was successively transferred,
to have encountered the neglects which con-

spicuous talent has often had to struggle with in
its outset. In more than one instance we have
seen that the esteem of others anticipated his
own modesty. We are little disposed to attribute
to accident any permanent success or popularity,
though the reader's recollection may furnish him
with one or more striking examples to the contrary. However this may be in political life, or
in other branches of affairs, "it is not at the bar,
at least," as Mr. Pinkney used to say, perhaps
with some conscious triumph, "that a man can
acquire or preserve a false and fraudulent reputation for talents." Fortune, indeed, as is commonly said, is wont to smile upon such as know
how to make a discreet use of her favours.

A fortunate occasion of this sort, for his professional fame, occurred in the year following
his removal to Richmond, when the celebrated
trial of Aaron Burr took place in that city, on a
charge which, deeply moving the interest and
passions of the whole nation, made familiar with
every person who could read a newspaper, all
the parties and actors in the cause. This trial
commenced in the winter of 1807, and Mr.
Wirt was retained, under the direction of President Jefferson, to aid the Attorney for the United
States in the prosecution. We believe it was

designed to engage him on the side of the prose-
cuted; but Mr. Wirt was absent from Richmond
at the moment, and no application was made to
him.

Few trials in any country ever excited a
greater sensation than this. The crime imputed
was of the deepest guilt; the accused, a person of the highest eminence both for talents and
political station, having but lately occupied the
second post, with pretensions to the first, in the
country the government of which he was charged
with a design to subvert. Conspicuous persons
were implicated in the supposed plot; and the
party violence which marked the period, mingled
itself in the opposite opinions which the transactions themselves might naturally create. Public
attention was consequently fixed with eager
curiosity on every step of the trial, and the counsel, the bench, and the government, scanned the
proceedings with the most inquisitive scrutiny.
The overt act of treason being charged to have
been committed within the jurisdiction of the
circuit court for the District of Virginia, the trial
was brought by this circumstance to the city of
Richmond, whose bar we have already mentioned to have been adorned by some of the first
men of the profession. The defence, which was

conducted by some of the most conspicuous of
these, derived additional aid from the legal learning of Luther Martin, who was familiarly called,
in his native state, "the law-leger," and not a
little from the legal acumen of the accused himself, whose great talents did not desert him on
this occasion.   A judge presided at the tribunal,
on whose intellectual vigour and moral dignity,
time and long trial have conferred a character of
grandeur.   The court was incessantly thronged
with earnest spectators and hearers, both from
Virginia and other states, many of them enlightened and conspicuous men.   It is evident that
this was not a theatre where, in the language of
Mr. Pinkney, a spurious reputation could be
supported, as, on the other hand, it gave scope
to the greatest reach of abilities.   It is justly
remarked by the reporter, a competent judge
that "perhaps no trial for treason has taken
place in any country, in which more ability,
learning, ingenuity and eloquence were displayed.
All the important decisions on treason in England and this country, were acutely and thoroughly examined, and their application to
questions before the court discussed with great
ingenuity and skill; nor was less industry or
judgment shown in arguing the application and

effect of the Constitution of the United States,
and of the common law, if it existed at all as a
law of the Union." The encomium of the Chief
Justice is as emphatic, and more authoritative.
" The question," says he, (speaking of one of
the principal arguments before the court,) " has
been argued in a manner worthy of its importance. A degree of eloquence seldom displayed
on any occasion, has embellished solidity of
argument and depth of research."

In a cause so vigorously urged and defended
Mr. Wirt enhanced and extended into every part
of the country, a reputation which is seldom
attained at thirty-five. His principal speech,
which occupied four hours, was replete throughout with a creative fancy, polished wit, keen
repartee, or logical reasoning; it is especially
marked by that comprehensiveness of thought
which " travels beyond the record," and brings
illustrations, analogies and aid from universal
reason and abstract truth. This diffuses a dignity and force over the production which his
technical learning, which is abundant and apt,
could not have bestowed alone. The diction
is chaste, never redundant; and he here displays
conspicuously that lucid order which is perhaps
the most remarkable quality of his eloquence;

the texture of the whole oration happily showing that in this sense the saying of Seneca is
untrue, " Non est ornamentum virile, concinni-
tas." One well-known popular passage in this
speech has shared the fate of many a classic
page, of palling by familiar repetition.

But we might quote several others as very
happy examples of oratorical skill ; the exordium,
in which he repels the charge repeatedly urged,
of personality and persecution to the accused ;
and the passage in which he describes the rhetorical arts employed against him by the opposite
counsel, Mr. Wickham. In his argument on
the motion to commit Burr and others for trial
in Kentucky, a vein of ridicule enlivens and
enforces the reasoning into which the picture of
the blasted ambition and daring despair of Burr
is inwoven with great effect.

We may add, in taking leave of this celebrated cause, that the excitements of the period
which gave it so much of its interest with the
public, elicited from the counsel themselves something more than the ordinary keenness of forensic debate. Readiness, firmness, and a large
portion of that civic courage which is perhaps the
most commanding quality of mind, were perpetually struck out in a proceeding in which the

whole public erected itself into a tribunal, or
rather took sides with all the eagerness of par-
tisans.

In 1808, Mr. Wirt was elected, without any
canvass on his part, a member of the Virginia
House of Delegates for the city of Richmond.
This was the first and last time he ever sat in
any legislative body, preferring the more con-
genial or more necessary pursuits of his profession, from which neither his popularity nor the
suggestions of those who thought they saw in
politics a more conspicuous theatre of action,
prevailed on him to withdraw. He was one of
the special committee appointed by the House of
Delegates in that session, to whom were referred
certain resolutions touching our foreign relations,
and the measures of administration which grew
out of them at that exceedingly embarrassing
and critical period. The report of the committee
is from the pen of Mr. Wirt. It reviews ener-
getically and impartially the measures of the two
belligerents, the French edicts and the British
orders in council, and comments indignantly on
the tone of the British diplomacy towards America, especially on the impertinent and insulting
discrimination of Mr. Canning between the people of this country and their government. The

report vindicates the measures of Mr. Jefferson's administration in this crisis, and urges the support of them on the nation. In the preceding July he was one of a committee appointed by " the Friends of the Manufacturing Association" of Virginia, to prepare an address to the people of the state. This paper, which was published in the Richmond Enquirer, reviews the above mentioned measures of the belligerents, and deduces from their unhappy operation on our commerce the necessity of fostering domestic manufactures, to which it argues that the capital, resources and mechanical skill of the country were entirely adequate.

In the same year, 1808, he wrote the essays in the Enquirer signed " One of the People," addressed to the members of Congress who had joined in a protest against the nomination of Mr. Madison to the presidency. In these he pourtrays the character and services of that venerable statesman with a warmth and emphasis which, now that time has mellowed the asperity of the period, and the illustrious sage of the constitution reposes in honoured retirement, one wonders to think should ever have been necessary.

It must be the sentiment of all good natures, in reviewing this and similar periods of political heats—when their eager contentions have lost their edge, and when so many of the acutest and ablest minds find in the opposite opinions so keenly maintained, so much to be modified, explained or reconciled—to retrace their whole career with some humility on their own part, and great indulgence to contemporary actors. Of this feeling we hardly know a stronger and more affecting instance than in the two illustrious sages of Monticello and Quincy; nor one that reads a more salutary and magnanimous lesson to the fierce rivalries of politicians. It cannot be doubted that the same sentiment which, in the meditative period of life, approached to each other, these leaders and idols of two parties so earnest and so angry, must be shared in a large degree by the subordinate actors in the contentious scene. Such, at least, we believe to be the view which all better spirits cast back on this period of our domestic politics, when, indeed, our foreign relations were so perplexing and provoking as unavoidably to sharpen the bitterness of other dissensions. In reviewing these scenes, the author of the Life of Patrick Henry holds this candid language:

"It is not my function to decide between these parties; nor do I feel myself qualified for such an office. I have lived too near the times, and am conscious of having been too strongly excited by the feelings of the day, to place myself in the chair of the arbiter. It would, indeed, be no difficult task to present, under the engaging air of historic candour, the arguments on one side in an attitude so bold and commanding, and to exhibit those on the other under a form so faint and shadowy, as to beguile the reader into the adoption of my own opinions. But this would be unjust to the opposite party, and a disingenuous abuse of the confidence of the reader. Let us then remit the question to the historian of future ages; who, if the particular memory of the past times shall not be lost in those great events which seem preparing for the nation, will probably decide that, as in most family quarrels, both parties have been somewhat in the wrong."

In his discourse on the death of Adams and Jefferson, he puts this subject in a still more amiable and interesting point of light. The orator says,—

" There was one solace of the declining years of both these great men, which must not be passed. It is that correspondence which arose between them, after their retirement from public life. That correspondence, it is to be hoped, will be given to the world. If it ever shall, I speak from knowledge when I say, it will be found to be one of the most interesting and affecting that the world has ever seen. That "cold cloud" which had hung for a time over their friendship, passed away with the conflict out of which it had grown, and the attachment of their early life returned in all its force. They had both now bid adieu, a final adieu, to all public employments, and were done with all the agitating passions of life. They were dead to the ambitious world; and this correspondence resembles, more than any thing else, one of those conversations in the Elysium of the ancients, which the shades of the departed great were supposed by them to hold, with regard to the affairs of the world they had left. There are the same playful allusions to the points of difference that had divided their parties; the same mutual, and light, and unimpassioned raillery on their own past misconceptions and mistakes; the same mutual and just admiration and respect for their many virtues and services to mankind. That correspondence was to them both, one of the most genial employments of their old age; and it reads a lesson of wisdom on the bitterness of party spirit, by which the wise and the good will not fail to profit."

But this candid mood was far from prevailing at the period which we have reached in this biographical sketch. Questions of portentous magnitude agitated the nation, and called forth no less passion than talent. Mr. Jefferson was just about to leave the Presidential chair; under Mr. Madison who was to succeed him, the same policy was to be pursued, and the same strenuous opposition to be anticipated. Under these circumstances, when honest men of both sides naturally looked about for the most capable agents—with the high confidence of his party, and with abilities that might have led him to any political distinctions—Mr. Wirt, however interested in the questions of the times, and with a large knowledge of them derived from his familiarity with the events and actors, declined to abandon the path of professional life. Though urged to it by such as could the most competently estimate both the turn of his genius and the value of his services to the public, he seems sedulously to have constrained himself from this bustling field within the calmer region of an intellectual pursuit, undazzled by the prospect of popular honours, though no man feels more the sting of a laudable ambition. Of those who saw in his capacity a broad foundation for fame in this new department of affairs, was his friend Mr. Jefferson, who, about the time of his own retirement, in language equally complimental of Mr. Wirt, and indicative of his profound interest in the crisis approaching under his successor, pointed out to him this career as equally worthy of his ambition and advantageous to the public, and one of which he might expect to bear off the first honours. His expressions denote as large a share of admiration and esteem as the ambition of any man can desire. One of the last acts, indeed, of Mr. Jefferson's life was an offer to Mr. Wirt on the part of the University of Virginia, accompanied by some circumstances that particularly evinced the respect he was held in by himself and the rest of that body.

From this period, therefore, till 1817, Mr. Wirt continued to practise law in Richmond and its vicinity, and we have little to record of the interval except his increasing reputation. During this period he gained several suits of particular celebrity and interest. In 1812 he wrote the series of papers entitled "The Old Bachelor." They were originally published in the Richmond Enquirer, and have since, in a collected form, passed through several editions. They are now republished, for the fourth time, in the ensuing volumes. It would appear from the second number, that the immediate occasion of them was the review of Ashe's Travels in America, in the thirtieth number of the Edinburgh Review; a well known scandalous libel on American institutions, manners and literature, in a periodical whose flippancy often exceeded even its wit. There were various contributors; but much the larger part of the papers were furnished by Mr. Wirt, and, like those in the Spy, were hastily thrown together in brief hours of relaxation.

The "Life of Patrick Henry," a work contemplated for some years, but put aside by professional pursuits, and eventually completed amidst the incessant hurry of them, was pub-

lished in September, 1817.   This is the longest,
and, judging by its whole effect on the reader,
the best of Mr. Wirt's literary productions.   Mr.
Jefferson's praise of it is the justest, and perhaps
the best an author can desire; that "those who
take up the book will find they cannot lay it
down, and this will be its best criticism."   Though
not included in the present publication, we have
some observations to make hereafter on this
work.   It had an extensive circulation, which
would have been greater yet but for circumstances having no connexion with its popularity
or literary merit.   In 1816 he was appointed, by
Mr. Madison, the Attorney of the United States
for the District of Virginia, and in the autumn
of the following year, by Mr. Monroe, Attorney-
General of the United States.   Both these ap-
pointments were unsolicited and unexpected by
him.   In consequence of the latter, he removed
in the winter of 1817–18 to Washington.

At the bar of the Supreme Court he found the
highest forensic theatre in the country, and perhaps there never was one in any country that
presented a more splendid array of learning and
talents conjoined.   In the causes, too, which it
is the official duty of the Attorney-General to
prosecute or defend, the most conspicuous coun

sel of that bar are commonly combined against
him.   In how many conflicts he sustained these
odds against him, with a vigour always adequate
to the occasion, is very well known to those who
are familiar with our judicial history.   The
office of Attorney-General he held twelve years,
through the entire administrations of Mr. Monroe
and Mr. Adams,—longer by many years than
it has ever been held by any other; and in this
post, always arduous, his labours seem much to
have surpassed those of his predecessors. Scarcely
any of them resided at Washington, nor did they
act as members of the cabinet.   They left no
written precedents nor opinions, nor any other
trace of their official course, to aid their successors.
Mr. Wirt, on the contrary, left behind him three
large volumes of official opinions.   His practice
soon became large in the Supreme Court, and with
it his celebrity as a profound jurist no less than an
orator of the first rank of his contemporaries. A
friend has remarked of him that his diligent
labour well deserved this success.   " He was
always," he says, "a man of labour; occasionally
of most intense and unremitting labour. He was
the most *improving* man, also, I ever knew ;
for I can truly say that I never heard him speak
after any length of time, without being surprised

and delighted at his improvement both in manner and substance." This testimony of an old
intimate, a man of parts and discernment, is
quoted as well for the praise it conveys, as in
proof of the unrelaxing toil by which men must
gain judicial eminence. Mr. Pinkney was to
the end of his days a model of this indefatigable
labour, and died, as it were, in the very act of
struggle.

At the close of Mr. Adams's administration,
Mr. Wirt, having resigned the Attorney-Generalship, removed to Baltimore, where he now
resides. He had been previously selected by the
citizens of Washington, on the death of Mr.
Jefferson and Mr. Adams, to pronounce a discourse on the lives and characters of those two
remarkable men ; this was delivered on the nineteenth of October, 1826. It contains several
passages of a strain altogether worthy of one
of the most impressive occasions that ever happened in any age or country. In 1830 he delivered an address to one of the literary societies
at Rutgers' College, and another in the same
year, at the celebration in Baltimore of the triumph of liberty in France. These various discourses have been printed, and are in the hands
of the public.

It remains to add to this sketch of Mr. Wirt's professional career, some notice of him as an orator and a writer, in which latter capacity he is presented in the ensuing publication. This contains, indeed, but his fugitive essays, the effusions rather of haste than leisure. The more strenuous efforts of his mind are to be sought in his forensic arguments, a great portion of which will share the fate of the labours of other great lawyers, and live only in the tradition of his hearers, and the admiring report of the day. Such, it is to be lamented, has been the fate of the greater part of the displays of Mr. Pinkney. The report of Burr's trial is in many hands however, and in the speeches of Mr. Wirt in that case the jurist will applaud more his extensive learning and comprehensive reasoning, than popular readers the more adorned and familiar passages. Others of his arguments, on questions of law or great constitutional principles, may still be preserved, and we hope will be collected. Among his writings not mentioned before, are the essays published in the Richmond Enquirer in 1809, under the signature of " The Sentinel," which throw light on some of the debated questions of the day. The essays in the following volumes, the interludes of graver business, apart

from their intrinsic merit, may have some further
curiosity as the recreations of a mind more than
usually engrossed by the toils of the most laborious of professions. In a criticism of " The
Old Bachelor," written some years ago by an
accomplished scholar and critic, the writer observes, " We look with gratitude and wonder
upon a gentleman of the bar, in whom the
severest labours, and highest offices, and amplest
emoluments, and brightest laurels of his profession, have not stifled the generous ambition of
letters; whose mind has been for a long term
of years exposed to the atmosphere of the courts,
and the attrition of the world of business, without losing any of the finer poetical qualities
with which it was richly endowed."*

" The British Spy" obtained, on its first appearance, the most flattering proof of merit,
popularity, which, to judge from its nine editions,
it has continued to retain. The story of the
Blind Preacher was almost as current as those
of Le Fevre and La Roche. The sketches of
character, a difficult department of good writing,
were esteemed so highly descriptive, in the cir-

* Review of " The Old Bachelor;" Analectic Magazine,
October, 1818.

cles where the depicted orators were known, as
to be in every hand. This kind of literature
was little practised among us when these essays
appeared ; and if they were the more kindly
received on that account, they have not however
been succeeded, in a period of nearly thirty years,
by any others of equal merit, of the same stamp.
" The Old Bachelor" seems, like its predecessor,
to have obtained an unexpected popularity. The
critic just quoted, says of these essays, " they
constitute one of the most successful experiments
which have been made in this department of letters since the era of Johnson." The disquisitions on eloquence, " originally," says the author,
" a prominent figure in his design," are those,
perhaps, which display most vigour, are imbued
the deepest with observation and thought, and
best show the influence on the author's mind,
of his familiar reading of the ancient classics.
The reader would be glad to see this topic re-
sumed and expanded by one who may remind
him, in some of the better passages, of the graceful composition imputed to Tacitus, " The Dialogue concerning Oratory."

Both these series of essays give a general
impression that, had the author devoted himself
to letters, he would have reached some of the

first excellences of writing. His conceptions
are vigorous and plentiful, his sentiments elevated and warm; his fancy, if it sometimes
betrays him into hyperbole, is generally delicate
and natural, and varies from grave to gay,
though not with equal facility in both. He is
serious and fervent for the most part; but some
of his best papers are those which, in the midst
of their earnestness and even warmth, have a
dash of good humour that shows he could have
played easily and cheerfully with his subject.
An example of this is in the third letter of the
Spy, where, exposing the " cold conceit of the
Roman division of a speech," he describes ludicrously the bustle of the modern orator when he
reaches the peroration, where by established
usage he is expected to be sublime or pathetic.
This " hysterical vehemence" is sketched from
life, with the felicity of Steele or Addison. The
same vein of humorous description appears in the
thirty-first and thirty-second numbers of the Old
Bachelor, and one of the illustrative anecdotes
would shine in a new treatise *peri bathous.*
This sort of painting, though in so different a
style, might be expected from a hand from which
we have the inspired sketch of the Blind
Preacher.

The mere diction of these essays is for the most part what he himself describes as a good one, " simple, pure and transparent, like the atmosphere, which never answers its purpose so well to make objects seen, as when free from vapours of every kind." But though this medium is never itself misty or obscure, it is now and then the vehicle of images somewhat meteoric and glaring. His redundancy, however, is not that of words, but of the thought, " vivo gurgite exundans ;" nor is it the redundancy of weakness, nor often of wrong taste, but that which is incident to hurried composition. His images, therefore, are frequently natural and elegant. Of the figure of amplification, we had admired the beginning of the twenty-third number of the Old Bachelor as a very happy example, when we found it mentioned in the same light in the criticism already quoted. The moral tone of the writer, and the " amiable fire" with which he paints virtue and inculcates her lessons, merit the most emphatic praise, as being the chief characteristic and aim of all his productions. Indeed this amiable temper meets us at every turn ; and to that quality, and not to any mawkish affectation of sentiment, is to be referred much of the warm colouring of some of his descriptions. He looks on the bright side of nature and human life; a turn of mind in a lawyer of two score years of practice, that indicates a large original fund of candour, generosity and good nature. It must be mentioned that some of the best papers of the Old Bachelor are from other hands; of this number are the twenty-fifth, twenty-ninth and thirty-third, and the letters in the fifteenth and twenty-first.

If we were to select a single passage from Mr. Wirt's writings in which he has most successfully addressed our moral passions, and called in the beauty and grandeur of external nature to heighten the effect, it would be the description in the discourse upon Adams and Jefferson, of the habitations and domestic habits of these two civic heroes. In that of Monticello, the reader is so skilfully wrought up by the mute majesty of the material images which the orator has been gradually assembling around him, that he sympathetically starts at the announcement of the "time-honoured" habitant of the spot. We do not fear to trespass on the reader by quoting the whole passage.

"Of 'the chief of the Argonauts,' as Mr. Jefferson so classically and so happily styled his illustrious friend of the North, it is my misfortune to be able to speak only by report. But every representation concurs, in drawing the same pleasing and affecting picture of the Roman simplicity in which that Father of his Country lived; of the frank, warm, cordial, and elegant reception that he gave to all who approached him; of the interesting kindness with which he disbursed the golden treasures of his experience, and shed around him the rays of his descending sun. His conversation was rich in anecdote and characters of the times that were past; rich in political and moral instruction: full of that best of wisdom, which is learnt from real life, and flowing from his heart with that warm and honest frankness, that fervour of feeling and force of diction, which so strikingly distinguished him in the meridian of his life. Many of us heard that simple and touching account given of a parting scene with him, by one of our eloquent divines : When he rose up from that little couch behind the door, on which he was wont to rest his aged and weary limbs, and with his silver locks hanging on each side of his honest face, stretched forth that pure hand, which was never soiled even by a suspicion, and gave his kind and parting benediction. Such was the blissful and honoured retirement of the sage of Quincy. Happy the life, which, verging upon a century, had met with but one serious political disappointment! and for that, too, he had lived to receive a golden atonement. 'Even there where he had garnered up his heart.'

"Let us now turn for a moment to the patriot of the South. The Roman moralist, in that great work which he has left for the government of man in all the offices of life, has descended even to prescribe the kind of habitation in which an honoured and distinguished man should dwell. It should not, he says, be small, and mean, and sordid: nor, on the other hand, extended with profuse and wanton extravagance. It should be large enough to receive and accommodate the visiters which such a man never fails to attract, and suited in its ornaments, as well as its dimensions, to the character and fortune of the individual. Monticello has now lost its great charm. Those of you who have not already visited it, will not be very apt to visit it hereafter: and, from the feelings which you cherish for its departed owner, I persuade myself that you will not be displeased with a brief and rapid sketch of that abode of domestic bliss, that temple of science. Nor is it, indeed, foreign to the express purpose of this meeting, which, in looking to 'his life and character,' naturally embraces his home and his domestic habits. Can any thing be indifferent to us, which was so dear to him, and which was a subject of such just admiration to the hundreds and thousands that were continually resorting to it, as to an object of pious pilgrimage?

"The Mansion House at Monticello was built and furnished in the days of his prosperity. In its dimensions, its architecture, its arrangements and ornaments, it is such a one as became the character and fortune of the man. It stands upon an elliptic plain, formed by cutting down the apex of a mountain; and, on the west, stretching away to the north and the south, it commands a view of the Blue Ridge for a hundred and fifty miles, and brings under the eye one of the boldest and most beautiful horizons in the world: while, on the east, it presents an extent of prospect bounded only by the spherical form of the earth, in which nature seems to sleep in eternal repose, as if to form one of her finest contrasts with the rude and rolling grandeur on the west. In the wide prospect, and scattered to the north and south, are several detached mountains, which contribute to animate and diversify this enchanting landscape; and among them, to the south, Willis's Mountain, which is so interestingly depicted in his Notes. From this summit, the Philosopher was wont to enjoy that spectacle, among the sublimest of Nature's operations, the looming of the distant mountains; and to watch the motions of the planets, and the greater revolution of the celestial sphere. From this summit, too, the patriot could look down, with uninterrupted vision, upon the wide expanse of the world around, for which he considered himself born; and upward, to the open and vaulted heavens which he seemed to approach, as if to keep him continually in mind of his high responsibility. It is indeed a prospect in which you see and feel, at once, that nothing mean or little could live. It is a scene fit to nourish those great and high-souled principles which formed the elements of his character, and was a most noble and appropriate post for such a sentinel, over the rights and liberties of man.

"Approaching the house on the east, the visiter instinctively paused, to cast around one thrilling glance at this magnificent panorama: and then passed to the vestibule, where, if he had not been previously informed, he would immediately perceive that he was entering the house of no common man. In the spacious and lofty hall which opens before him, he marks no tawdry and unmeaning ornaments: but before, on the right, on the left, all around, the eye is struck and gratified with objects of science and taste, so classed and arranged as to produce their finest effect. On one side, specimens of sculpture set out, in such order, as to exhibit at a *coup d'œil*, the historical progress of that art; from the first rude attempts of the aborigines of our country, up to that exquisite and finished bust of the great patriot himself, from the master hand of Caracci. On the other side, the visiter sees displayed a vast collection of specimens of Indian art, their paintings, weapons, ornaments, and manufactures; on another, an array of the fossil productions of our country, mineral and animal; the polished remains of those colossal monsters that once trod our forests, and are no more; and a variegated display of the branching honours

of those 'monarchs of the waste,' that still people the wilds
of the American Continent.

"From this hall he was ushered into a noble saloon, from
which the glorious landscape of the west again bursts upon
his view; and which, within, is hung thick around with the
finest productions of the pencil—historical paintings of the
most striking subjects from all countries, and all ages; the
portraits of distinguished men and patriots, both of Europe
and America and medallions and engravings in endless
profusion.

"While the visiter was yet lost in the contemplation of
these treasures of the arts and sciences, he was startled by
the approach of a strong and sprightly step, and turning
with instinctive reverence to the door of entrance, he was
met by the tall, and animated, and stately figure of the patriot himself—his countenance beaming with intelligence
and benignity, and his outstretched hand, with its strong
and cordial pressure, confirming the courteous welcome of his
lips. And then came that charm of manner and conversation that passes all description—so cheerful—so unassuming
—so free, and easy, and frank, and kind, and gay—that
even the young, and overawed, and embarrassed visiter·at
once forgot his fears, and felt himself by the side of an old
and familiar friend."

In the "Life of Patrick Henry," though a
work of Mr. Wirt's more mature age, the manner of the narrative has been thought too ambitious, and the subject of it to be decked in the
colours of declamation and fancy. These are
faults to repel the judicious reader; yet the volume is not one which the most judicious will

lay down unfinished, or will read with weari-
ness. It often occurred to us, we confess, in our
first perusal of this work, that the hero of it
seemed more like the creation of a rhetorician,
than a personage of history, however grave, eloquent and eminent in the view of his contemporaries; and, in common with others of the
author's readers, we gave him credit for having
filled up his drawing with colours over rich and
splendid. Yet when we referred again to the
incidents and anecdotes, and found them often
told in the words of the relaters; when we recollected, however vaguely the causes might be
assigned, there was a general concurrence as to
the effects of this traditionary eloquence; we
began to think that the exaggeration, if any,
was that of the witnesses and not of the advocate
in the cause. Nor will it account for this lavish
praise, that these orations, so celebrated in Virginia, were addressed, as has been said, to the
more popular kinds of assemblies, " whose feelings are easily excited, and whose opinions are
seldom founded on the basis of rational conviction."* This is not true of a large portion of
these efforts; on the contrary, the auditors who

---

*North American Review for March, 1818.

are witnesses in the case, were many of them
men not only of the first eminence in their own
state, but famous throughout the continent, and
some of them themselves the men of posterity.
Mr. Jefferson, who is surely one of the latter
class, uses language that justifies the boldest
praise of the biographer, and proves that the
powers of Henry were felt alike by all degrees
both of condition and discernment. That eminent man is cited, it may be remembered, as
authority for many passages in the work; and
in some of his letters communicating information
to the author, he is known to have spoken of the
oratory of Henry as " bold, grand and overwhelming," giving " examples of eloquence such
as probably had never been exceeded," and the
man himself as having been "the idol of his state,"
beyond example. Of the same tone is the evidence of many other persons whose celebrity is
some warrant of their good taste; and many
authentic anecdotes are afloat, some of them odd
enough, and not such as to find place in a serious
work, which would show what an extraordinary
impression prevailed in his native state, of the
command of this memorable person over the reason as well as the passions of men. Of one of
these great displays the old Congress was the

theatre; an assembly compared with the most venerable senates of ancient or modern days, by one who would himself have been the ornament of any; and yet the tradition of its effect is not less constant or emphatic.

No anecdotes, therefore, related of ancient eloquence are more authentic than those of the oratory of our illustrious countryman. Yet, when the modern reader, in an age too, as has been sarcastically observed, when writing and printing are not unknown, asks for even the fragments of this splendid web, and finds them few and meager, he is inclined to regard the evidence with some disbelief, and the writer who reflects its warmth in his work, as credulous and declamatory. But such a conclusion is to disregard unjustifiably a cloud of judicious contemporary witnesses on the one hand, and on the other, to forget with what imperfect remains, carelessly preserved, mutilated and defaced by the collectors, and never repaired by the hand of the original designer, we are to compare their descriptions. Of the greater part of these orations we have only such fragments as could be carried away in the memory of the hearers, who, however fit to estimate their excellence as critics, might not have the faculty nor the occasion to relate them correctly. Of those, again, more regularly reported, as in the debates of the Virginia Convention, it is a striking and very curious circumstance, that the reporter seems to have " dropped" Mr. Henry, to use his biographer's expression, in those very passages where the reader would be most anxious to follow him. So in the stenographical notes of the argument on the British debts, it is, as the biographer informs us, where we are prepared for the most captivating or overwhelming flights, that the frequent erasures bear most marks of an apparent but ineffectual effort to recall what the enchantment of the moment caused to escape the verbal record of the reporter. Attentively considered, this circumstance, which deprives us of the language of the orator, is another of the many homages of his hearers to his enchanting faculty.

Recollecting and weighing these circumstances, we doubt whether the author of the Life of Patrick Henry has done more in his fervid delineation of him, than reflect the united testimony of witnesses of all classes, whether friends or foes. Had he, in fact, practised a rhetorical art; had he seemed to kindle less himself in bringing these glowing traditions before his reader, and in reality heightened their effect by a kind of reluctant exhibition of their energy and unanimousness, we are tempted to think he would more completely have won the conviction which we cannot reasonably withhold from the evidence he has adduced. The same thing seems true of the companion-pieces of the principal portrait. They were a body of men altogether remarkable and splendid, and Mr. Jefferson, through whose hands the author's manuscript passed, declares the characters to be " inimitably and justly drawn." Tradition, it must be remarked, so uniform in respect to Mr. Henry's oratory is no less so as to his defects ; and it is another vindication of the biographer's impartiality, that these are noted without hesitation in his memoir. In both he echoed the voice of contemporaries, and in regard to his eloquence, only joined in a general acclaim.

These observations are exceeding our limits, or we might remark it as somewhat curious, that the " action" which Demosthenes has been thought to have disproportionably lauded, and which, by universal concurrence, formed the secret and chief charm of Patrick Henry's elocution, has in some sort caused his pretensions to be doubted. Unwilling to impute such extraordinary effects to such a cause, we prefer to reject

at once both the judgment of the Greek orator
and this modern evidence of its truth; thus
denying to the critic the confirmation of the example, and to the example the authority of the
critic. There are, however, brief passages of
Henry's, as they are given in his life, which,
mutilated as they have come down to us, are
worthy of Chatham, and worthy of any orator,
in any age. The biography, we think, is not
likely to perish either from want of interest in its
subject, or of skill in the writer, who, without
alteration of the facts—which, besides the popular belief, we have the venerable authority
already quoted, that he took great pains " to sift
and scrutinize,"—but by subduing the warm
tone of the narrative, may render it an enduring
portion of our popular literature. The subject
has been pursued to such length, however,
chiefly from its interest as a general question.

In taking leave of it we may add the opinion
of a writer* who, though snatched away in the
morning of a promising day, may be cited on a
subject which he has treated with no less knowledge than eloquence. The passage is equally
complimentary to Patrick Henry and Mr. Wirt.

---

* The late Francis Walker Gilmer.

"Had one," he says, " with so rich a genius, with such a soul for eloquence, as Mr. Wirt certainly possesses, seen Mr. Henry in some of his grandest exhibitions, I should not now have to deplore the want of a finished orator at any American bar. But that bright meteor shot from its mid-heaven sphere too early for Mr. Wirt, and the glory of his art descended with him." As the most effective and correct description of Mr. Wirt's oratory to which we can add nothing, and which we should be unwilling to retrench, we extract the remainder of this passage, though it is probably familiar to many. The reader may recollect that the elocution of Mr. Wirt was originally faulty in several particulars. Of these defects his nice ear and good taste rendered him painfully sensible, and he bent himself determinedly to the cure of them ; with what success will appear from Mr. Gilmer's picture of him.

"But I have seen no one who has such natural advantages and so many qualities requisite for genuine eloquence as Mr. Wirt. His person is dignified and commanding; his countenance open, manly and playful; his voice clear and musical; and his whole appearance truly oratorical. Judgment and imagination hold a divided dominion over his mind, and each is so conspicuous that it is difficult to decide which is ascendant. His diction unites force, purity, variety and splendour, more perfectly than that of any speaker I have heard, except Mr. Pinkney. He had great original powers of action, but they have been totally unassisted by the contemplation of a good model. His wit is prompt, pure, and brilliant, but these lesser scintillations of fancy are lost in the blaze of his reasoning and declamation.

" His premises are always broad and distinctly laid down, his deductions are faultless, and his conclusions of course, irresistible from the predicate. In this he resembles what he has observed of Mr. Marshall, admit his first proposition and the conclusion is inevitable. The march of his mind is direct to its object, the evolutions by which he attains it, are so new and beautiful, and apparently necessary to the occasion, that your admiration is kept alive, your fancy delighted, and your judgment convinced, through every stage of the process. He leaves no objection to his reasoning unanswered, but satisfies every doubt as he advances. His power over his subject is so great, and so judiciously directed, that he sweeps the whole field of discussion, rarely leaves any thing for his assistants to glean, and sometimes anticipating the position of his enemy's battery, renders it useless, by destroying before-hand the materials of which its fortifications were to be erected. He has been sometimes known to answer, by anticipation, all the arguments of the opposing counsel so perfectly, as to leave him nothing to say which had not been better said already. These great combinations are so closely connected, the succession of their parts so natural, easy, and rapid, that the whole operation, offensive and defensive, appears but one effort. There is no weak point in his array, no chink in the whole line of his extended works. Then the sweet melody of voice, the beautiful decorations of fancy, the easy play of a powerful reason, by which all this is accomplished, amaze and delight. His pathos is natural and impressive; there is a pastoral simplicity and tenderness in his pictures of distress, when he describes female innocence, helplessness, and beauty, which the husband on whom she smiled should have guarded even from the winds of heaven which might visit it too roughly, "shivering at midnight on the winter banks of the Ohio, and mingling her tears with the torrent, which froze as they fell;" it is not a theatrical trick, to move a fleeting pity, but a deep and impressive appeal to the dignified charities of our nature."*

An opinion prevailed perhaps, at one time, that it was rather in the ornate than the severer qualities of oratory that Mr. Wirt excelled. Except indeed that some of his brilliancies, if we may call them so, found their way into popular works, there was, perhaps, no better reason for supposing a person who wrote with taste, and spoke with force and feeling, on that account to want argument, than for the converse in the case of the attorney, who, as the jest goes, was reported to be a great lawyer because he was a miserable speaker. Those who knew him the earliest, concur that the striking feature of his mind " was the power of argument, of close, connected, cogent, logical reasoning." In the unforeseen points that arise before a court, where the argument of counsel must be instant and extemporaneous, he was always eminent for ready force as well as for lucid order. The writer remembers

---

* Gilmer's Sketches, &c. pp. 38, 39.

the first forensic encounter between him and Mr.
Pinkney, in Baltimore, and the impression also
of his speech compared with that of his formidable rival. If, to use an old figure, he was struck
by the elaborate Gothic beauties of the one, he
drew a calmer pleasure from the Grecian elegance and proportions of the other, where grace
was subservient to utility, and all the parts were
happily disposed toward the main design. In
the structure of his speeches there is much of
what Quintilian calls the " apta junctura." He
seemed, however, in his own words, " not deco-
rated for pomp, but armed for battle." Yet this
opinion of his ornament, " scilicet nimia facilitas
magis quam facultas," appeared to have been
somewhat diffused ; for it is not long since an
eminent judge, on first hearing the advocate
in some cause of moment, observed to him that
he did not know till then that he was a logician.
The well known description of Blennerhasset
and his Island has been thought no more than
the creation of the orator's fancy. But it is as
well known to many, that the evidence on which
that passage of the speech was founded, (which
does not appear in the report of the trial,) was
quite as high-wrought in the description. In
fine, we may appositely quote on this subject, a

passage in the Dialogue concerning Oratory.
The unknown but graceful writer says of some of
Cicero's earlier orations, " Firmus sane paries, et
duraturus, sed non satis expolitus et splendens;"
and he continues the figure naturally, " Non eo
tantum volo tecto tegi, quod imbrem ac ven-
tum arceat, sed etiam quod visum et oculos
delectet."

Mr. Wirt has appeared in causes in Philadelphia and Boston. Of his many arguments
before the Supreme Court it is not our purpose
to speak ; but an extract may not be unacceptable from a speech in what will be recollected as
the "steam-boat case," decided by that court in
1824. It was a cause of deep interest, and important not only from the nature of the individual
rights involved, but on account of the collisions
which gave rise to it, of the state of New-York,
with those of Connecticut and New Jersey. The
arguments of counsel,—Webster and Wirt for
the appellant, Oakly and Emmet for the appel-
lee,—were most able and profound, and the
papers of the day, which were much occupied
with the cause, dwelt with emphasis on the
ability of the Attorney-General's speech, particularly of the concluding passages, in which with
rare felicity he had retorted on his eminent

antagonist, Mr. Emmet, a quotation of the latter from Virgil.

The Attorney-General observed, that his learned friend (Mr. Emmet) had eloquently personified the state of New-York, casting her eyes over the ocean, witnessing every where the triumph of her genius, and exclaiming, in the language of Æneas,

" 'Quæ regio in terris, nostri non plenæ laboris ?'

"Sir, it was not in the moment of triumph, nor with the feelings of triumph, that Æneas uttered that exclamation. It was when, with his faithful Achates by his side, he was surveying the works of art with which the palace of Carthage was adorned, and his attention had been caught by a representation of the battles of Troy. There he saw the sons of Atreus, and Priam, and the fierce Achilles. The whole extent of his misfortunes ; the loss and desolation of his friends ; the fall of his beloved country ; rushed upon his recollection.

'Constitit et lachrymans, quis jam locus, inquit, Achate,
    Quæ regio in terris, nostri non plenæ laboris ?'

"Sir, the passage may hereafter have a closer application to the cause than my eloquent and classical friend intended. For if the state of things which has already commenced, is to go on ; if the spirit of hostility which already exists in three of our states, is to catch by contagion, and spread among the rest, as, from the progress of the human passions, and the unavoidable conflict of interests, it will too surely do ; what are we to expect ? Civil wars, arising from far inferior causes, have desolated some of the fairest provinces of the earth. History is full of the afflicting narratives of such wars; and it will continue to be her mournful office to record them, till 'time shall be no longer.' It is a momentous decision which this court is called on to make. Here are three states almost on the eve of war. It is the high province of this court to interpose its benign and mediatorial influence. The framers of our admirable constitution would have deserved the wreath of immortality which they have acquired, had they done nothing else than to establish this guardian tribunal, to harmonize the jarring elements in our system. But, sir, if you do not interpose your friendly hand, and extirpate the seeds of anarchy which New-York has sown, you *will* have civil war. The war of legislation which has already commenced, will, according to its usual course, become a war of blows. Your country will be shaken with civil strife. Your republican institutions will perish in the conflict. Your constitution will fall. The last hope of nations will be gone. And what will be the effect upon the rest of the world? Look abroad at the scenes now passing on our globe, and judge of that effect. The friends of free government throughout the earth, who have been heretofore animated by our example, and have cheerfully cast their glance to it, as to their polar star, to guide them through the stormy seas of revolution, will witness our fall, *with dismay and despair*. The arm that is every where lifted in the cause of liberty, will drop unnerved by the warrior's side. Despotism will have its day of triumph, and will accomplish the purpose at which it too certainly aims. It will cover the earth with the mantle of mourning. *Then*, sir, when New-York shall look upon this scene of ruin, if she have the generous feelings which I believe her to have, it will not be with her head aloft, in the pride of conscious triumph, ' her rapt soul sitting in her eyes.'—No, sir, no! Dejected with shame and confusion, drooping under the weight of her sorrow, with a voice suffocated with despair, *well* may she *then* exclaim,

> " '——————— Quis jam locus, ———
> Quæ regio in terris, nostri non plenæ laboris ?' "

Mr. Wirt has just entered his sixtieth year, and still resides in Baltimore, an eminent ornament of a state which may number with some pride among her sons, a Dulany, a Chase, a Martin, and a Pinkney. For the narrative given in the preceding pages, we have the brief apology of the classic: " hujus vitam narrare, fiduciam potius morum, quam arrogantiam."

———————

The subject of the above memoir has acquired a new interest with the public from his nomination by the Anti-Masonic Convention, assembled at Baltimore in October last, as a candidate for the Presidency of the United States ; an eminence to which he brings the pretensions of pure morals and native dignity; of a high intellect, clear, vigorous and direct, refined by knowledge, and by a large acquaintance with mankind, especially with the eminent talents of his age ; of profound constitutional learning, and of an intimate knowledge of the points and course of our national policy, acquired during a period of twelve years, during which, in the capacity of Attorney-General, he held a seat in the cabinet. No man has more integrity in private life, and none would bring into the administration of public affairs a more sincere, candid, elevated or patriotic purpose. Though, restrained by personal and professional considerations, he has never mingled in the competitions of politics, he has spoken and written on many of the questions which have agitated and divided the public opinion. Such a mind, with such opportunities and occasions of observation, must have cast over the whole field of our policy, that broad and comprehensive glance which justifies this recent proof of the confidence of a considerable portion of the public.

THE

LETTERS

OF THE

BRITISH SPY.

THE publishers having become possessed of a copy of "The British Spy," which has passed through the hands of the author, eagerly embrace an opportunity of submitting a correct edition of that work to the patronage of the public. These letters were originally inserted in a daily journal; and they appeared with all the imperfections to which such a mode of publication is unavoidably liable. In the present edition, a variety of errors have been corrected; and nothing has been spared which it was supposed could add to its value.

Of the literary merit of a work which has passed the ordeal of criticism with honour, not only to the author but to his country, it would be impertinent to speak. Common fame has decided it to be the fruit of an American pen;

and classical taste has pronounced it to be the offspring of genius. To those who would inculcate the degrading doctrine, that this is the country

" Where Genius sickens, and where Fancy dies,"*

we would offer the letters of the British Spy as an unquestionable evidence that America is entitled to a high rank in the republic of letters; and that the empyreal flame may be respired under any region.

* Clifton.

Sir,

THE manuscript, from which the following letters are extracted, was found in the bed-chamber of a boarding-house in a seaport town of Virginia. The gentleman, who had previously occupied that chamber, is represented, by the mistress of the house, to have been a meek and harmless young man, who meddled very little with the affairs of others, and concerning whom no one appeared sufficiently interested to make any inquiry. As it seems from the manuscript that the name by which he passed was not his real name, and as, moreover, she knew nothing of his residence, so that she was totally ignorant to whom and whither to direct it, she considered the manuscript as lawful prize, and made a present of it to me. It seems to be a copy of letters written by a young Englishman of rank, during a tour through the United States, in 1803, to a member of the British parliament. They are dated from almost every part of the United States, contain a great deal of geographical description, a delineation of every character of note among us, some literary disquisitions, with a great mixture of moral and political observation.

The letters are prettily written. Persons of every description will find in them a light and agreeable entertainment; and to the younger part of your readers they may not be uninstructive. For the present I select a few which were written from this place, and by way of distinction, will give them to you under the title of the *British Spy*.

THE BRITISH SPY.

———

LETTER I.

Richmond, September 1.

You complain, my dear S . . . . , that although I have been resident in Richmond upward of six months, you have heard nothing from me since my arrival. The truth is, that I had suspended writing until a more intimate acquaintance with the people and their country should furnish me with the materials for a correspondence. Having now collected those materials, the apology ceases, and the correspondence begins. But first, a word of myself.

I still continue to wear the mask, and most willingly exchange the attentions, which would be paid to my rank, for the superior and exquisite pleasure of inspecting this country and this people, without attracting to myself a single eye of curiosity, or awakening a shade of suspicion. Under my assumed name, I gain an admission

close enough to trace, at leisure, every line of
the American character; while the plainness, or
rather humility of my appearance, my manners
and conversation, put no one on his guard, but
enable me to take the portrait of nature, as it
were, asleep and naked. Beside, there is something of innocent roguery in this masquerade,
which I am playing, that sorts very well with
the sportiveness of my temper. To sit and decoy
the human heart from behind all its disguises:
to watch the capricious evolutions of unrestrained
nature, frisking, curvetting and gambolling at
her ease, with the curtain of ceremony drawn
up to the very sky—Oh! it is delightful!

You are perhaps surprised at my speaking of
the attentions which would be paid in this
country to my rank. You will suppose that I
have forgotten where I am: no such thing. I
remember well enough that I am in Virginia,
that state, which, of all the rest, plumes herself
most highly on the democratic spirit of her principles. Her political principles are indeed democratic enough in all conscience. Rights and
privileges, as regulated by the constitution of the
state, belong in equal degree to all the citizens;
and Peter Pindar's remark is perfectly true of
the people of this country, that "every black-

guard scoundrel is a king."*   Nevertheless,
there exists in Virginia a species of social rank,
from which no country can, I presume, be entirely free.   I mean that kind of rank which
arises from the different degrees of wealth and
of intellectual refinement.   These must introduce
a style of living and of conversation, the former
of which a poor man cannot attain, while an
ignorant one would be incapable of enjoying the
latter.   It seems to me that from these causes,
wherever they may exist, circles of society,
strongly discriminated, must inevitably result.
And one of these causes exists in full force in
Virginia ; for, however they may vaunt of
" equal liberty in church and state," they have
but little to boast on the subject of equal property.
Indeed there is no country, I believe, where
property is more unequally distributed than in
Virginia.   This inequality struck me with peculiar force in riding through the lower counties
on the Potomac.   Here and there a stately aristocratic palace, with all its appurtenances, strikes
the view; while all around, for many miles, no
other buildings are to be seen but the little smoky
huts and log cabins of poor, laborious, ignorant

---

* The reader needs scarcely to be reminded that the writer
is a Briton, and true to his character.

tenants. And, what is very ridiculous, these
tenants, while they approach *the great house*,
cap in hand, with all the fearful, trembling sub-
mission of the lowest feudal vassals, boast in
their court-yards, with obstreperous exultation,
that they live in a land of freemen, a land of
equal liberty and equal rights. Whether this
debasing sense of inferiority, which I have mentioned, be a remnant of their colonial character,
or whether it be that it is natural for poverty and
impotence to look up with veneration to wealth,
and power, and rank, I cannot decide. For my
own part, however, I have ascribed it to the
latter cause; and I have been in a great degree
confirmed in the opinion, by observing the attentions which were paid by the most genteel people
here to . . . . . . the son of lord . . . .

You know the circumstances in which his
lordship left Virginia : that so far from being
popular, he carried with him the deepest execra-
tions of these people. Even now, his name is
seldom mentioned here but in connexion with
terms of abhorrence or contempt. Aware of
this, and believing it impossible that . . . . . .
was indebted to his father, for all the parade of
respect which was shown to him, I sought, in
his own personal accomplishments, a solution of

the phenomenon. But I sought in vain. Without
one solitary ray of native genius, without one
adventitious beam of science, without any of
those traits of soft benevolence which are so universally captivating, I found his mind dark and
benighted, his manners bold, forward and
assuming, and his whole character evidently
inflated with the consideration that he was the
son of a lord. His deportment was so evidently
dictated by this consideration, and he regarded
the Virginians so palpably, in the humiliating
light of inferior plebeians, that I have often
wondered how such a man, and the son too of
so very unpopular a father, escaped from this
country without personal injury, or, at least, personal insult. I am now persuaded, that this
impunity, and the great respect which was paid
to him, resulted solely from his noble descent,
and was nothing more than the tribute which
man pays either to imaginary or real superiority.
On this occasion, I stated my surprise to a young
Virginian, who happened to belong to the democratic party. He, however, did not choose to
admit the statement; but asserted, that whatever
respect had been shown to . . . . ,
proceeded solely from the federalists ; and that it
was an unguarded evolution of their private

attachment to monarchy and its appendages. I
then stated the subject to a very sensible gentleman, whom I knew to belong to the federal phalanx.   Not willing to degrade his party by
admitting that they would prostrate themselves
before the empty shadow of nobility, he alleged
that nothing had been manifested towards
young . . . . , beyond the hospitality
which was due to a genteel stranger ; and that
if there had been any thing of parade on his
account, it was attributable only to the ladies, who
had merely exercised their wonted privilege of
coquetting it with a fine young fellow.   But
notwithstanding all this, it was easy to discern
in the look, the voice, and whole manner, with
which gentlemen as well as ladies of both parties
saluted and accosted young . . . . , a
secret spirit of respectful diffidence, a species of
silent, reverential abasement, which, as it could
not have been excited by his personal qualities,
must have been homage to his rank.   Judge,
then, whether I have not just reason to apprehend, that on the annunciation of my real name,
the curtain of ceremony would fall, and nature
would cease to play her pranks before me.

Richmond is built, as you will remember, on the
north side of James river, and at the head of tide

water. There is a manuscript in this state which relates a curious anecdote concerning the origin of this town. The land hereabout was owned by Col. William Byrd. This gentleman, with the former proprietor of the land at the head of tide water on Appomatox river, was appointed, it seems, to run the line between Virginia and North Carolina. The operation was a most tremendous one ; for, in the execution of it, they had to penetrate and pass quite through the great Dismal Swamp. It would be almost impossible to give you a just conception of the horrors of this enterprise. Imagine to yourself an immense morass, more than forty miles in length and twenty in breadth, its soil a black, deep mire, covered with a stupendous forest of juniper and cypress trees, whose luxuriant branches, interwoven throughout, intercept the beams of the sun and teach day to counterfeit the night This forest, which until that time, perhaps, the human foot had never violated, had become the secure retreat of ten thousand beasts of prey. The adventurers, therefore, beside the almost endless labour of felling trees in a proper direction to form a footway throughout, moved amid perpetual terrors, and each night had to sleep *en militaire*, upon their arms, surrounded with the deafening, soul-chilling yell of those hunger-smitten lords of the desert. It was, one night, as they lay in the midst of scenes like these, that Hope, that never-failing friend of man, paid them a consoling visit, and sketched in brilliant prospect the plans of Richmond and Petersburg.*

Richmond occupies a very picturesque and most beautiful situation. I have never met with such an assemblage of striking and interesting objects. The town, dispersed over hills of various shapes; the river descending from west to east, and obstructed by a multitude of small islands, clumps of trees, and myriads of rocks; among which it tumbles, foams, and roars, constituting what are called the falls; the same river, at the lower end of the town, bending at right angles to the south, and winding reluctantly off for many miles in that direction! its polished surface caught here and there by the eye, but more generally covered from the view by trees; among which the white sails of approaching and departing vessels exhibit a curious and interesting appearance: then again, on the opposite

---

* So at least, speaks the manuscript account which Col. Byrd has left of this expedition, and which is now in the hands of some of his descendants; perhaps of the family at Westover.

side, the little town of Manchester, built on a
hill, which, sloping gently to the river, opens
the whole town to the view, interspersed, as it
is, with vigorous, and flourishing poplars, and
surrounded to a great distance by green plains
and stately woods—all these objects, falling at
once under the eye, constitute, by far, the most
finely varied and most animated landscape that
I have ever seen.   A mountain, like the Blue
Ridge, in the western horizon, and the rich tint
with which the hand of a Pennsylvanian farmer
would paint the adjacent fields, would make this
a more enchanting spot than even Demascus is
described to be.

I will endeavour to procure for you a perspec-
tive view of Richmond, with the embellishments
of fancy which I have just mentioned; and you
will do me the honour to give it a place in your
pavilion.

Adieu for the present, my dear S . . . . ,
May the perpetual smiles of heaven be yours.

LETTER II.

Richmond, September 7.

ALMOST every day, My dear S . . . . , some new evidence presents itself in support of the Abbe Raynal's opinion, that this continent was once covered by the ocean, from which it has gradually emerged. But that this emersion is, even comparatively speaking, of recent date, cannot be admitted ; unless the comparison be made with the creation of the earth ; and even then, in order to justify the remark, the era of the creation must, I fear, be fixed much further back than the period which has been inferred from the Mosaic account.*

---

* Some error has certainly happened in computing the era of the earth's creation from the five books of Moses. Voltaire informs us, that certain French philosophers, who visited China, inspected the official register or history of the eclipses of the sun and moon, which, it seems, has been continually kept in that country ; that on calculating them back, they were all found correct, and conducted those philosophers to a period, (I will not undertake to speak with certainty of the time, but I think,) twenty-three centuries before the Mosaic era. It is notorious, however, that the Chinese plume themselves on the antiquity of their country ; and in

The following facts are authenticated beyond any kind of doubt. During the last spring a gentleman in the neighbourhood of Williams-

---

order to prop this, it would have been just as easy for the Chinese astronomers to have fabricated and dressed up the register in question, by posterior calculations, as for the French astronomers to have made their retrospective examination of the accuracy of those eclipses. The same science precisely was requisite for both purposes; and although the improvement of the arts and sciences in China, was found by the first Europeans who went amongst them, to bear no proportion to the antiquity of the country, yet there is no reason to doubt that the Chinese mandarins were at least as competent to the calculation of an eclipse as the Shepherds of Egypt. Indeed we are, I believe, expressly told, that the Chinese, long before they were visited by the people of Europe, had been in the habit of using a species of astronomical apparatus; and of stamping almanacs from plates or blocks, many hundred years, even before printing was discovered in Europe. I see no great reason, therefore, to rely with very implicit confidence on the register of China. Indeed I am very little disposed to build my faith, as to any historical fact, on evidence perfectly within the reach of human art and imposture; comprehending all writings, inscriptions, literary or hieroglyphic, medals, &c. which tend either to flatter our passion for the marvellous, or aggrandize the particular nation in whose bosom they are found. And, therefore, together with the Chinese register, I throw out of the consideration of this question another record which goes to the same purpose; I mean the Chaldaic manuscript found by Alexander in the city of Babylon.

The inferences reported by Mr. Brydone, as having been

burg, about sixty miles below this place, in digging a ditch on his farm, discovered about four
or five feet below the surface of the earth, a con-

---

drawn by Recupero, from the *lavas* of mount Etna (those
stupendous records which no human art or imposture could
possibly have fabricated) deserve, I think, much more serious
attention.   They are subject, indeed, to one of the preceding
objections, to wit: that the data, from which all the subsequent
calculations are drawn, are inscriptions: appealing not only
to our passion for the marvellous, but flattering the vanity of
the Sicilians, by establishing the great age of their mountain,
at once their curse and their blessing.   These inscriptions,
however, do not rest merely on their own authority: they
allege a fact which is very strongly countenanced by recent
and unerring observation.   As Brydone may not be in the
hands of every person who may chance to possess and read
this *bagatelle*, and as this subject is really curious and interesting, I beg leave to subjoin those parts of that traveller's
nighly entertaining letters which relate to it.

"The last *lava* we crossed, before our arrival there (*Jaci
Reale*) is of vast extent.   I thought we never should have
had done with it; it certainly is not less than six or seven
miles broad, and appears in many places to be of an enormous depth.

"When we came near the sea, I was desirous to see what
form it had assumed in meeting with the water.   I went to
examine it, and found it had driven back the waves for
upward of a mile, and had formed a large, black, high prom-
ontory, where, before, it was deep water.   This *lava*, I
imagined, from its barrenness, for it is, as yet, covered with
a very scanty soil, had run from the mountain only a few
ages ago; but was surprised to be informed by Signor Recu-

siderable portion of the skeleton of a whale. Several fragments of the ribs and other parts of the system were found; and all the *vertebræ*

---

pero, the historiographer of Etna, that this very *lava* is mentioned by Diodorus Siculus to have burst from Etna in the time of the second Punic war, when Syracuse was besieged by the Romans. A detachment was sent from Taurominum to the relief of the besieged. They were stopped on their march by this stream of lava, which having reached the sea before their arrival at the foot of the mountain, had cut off their passage, and obliged them to return by the back of Etna, upwards of a hundred miles about. His authority for this, he tells me, was taken from inscriptions on Roman monuments found on this lava, and that it was likewise well ascertained by many of the old Sicilian authors. Now as this is about two thousand years ago, one would imagine, if *lavas* have a regular progress in becoming fertile fields, that this must long ago have become at least arable; this, however, is not the case: and it is, as yet, only covered with a very scanty vegetation, and incapable of producing either corn or vines. There are indeed pretty large trees growing in the crevices which are full of a rich earth; but in all probability, it will be some hundred years yet, before there is enough of it to render this land of any use to the proprietors.

" It is curious to consider, that the surface of this black and barren matter, in process of time, becomes one of the most fertile soils upon earth. But what must be the time to bring it to its utmost perfection, when after two thousand years, it is still, in most places, but a barren rock ?"— *Vol. I. Letter* 6.

" Signior Recupero, who obligingly engages to be our *cicerone*, has shown us some curious remains of antiquity;

regularly arranged and very little impaired as to their figure. The spot on which this skeleton was found, lies about two miles from the nearest shore of James river, and fifty or sixty from the Atlantic Ocean. The whole phenomenon bore the clearest evidence that the animal had perished in its native element; and as the ocean is the nearest resort of the whale, it follows that

---

but they have been all so shaken and shattered by the mountain, that hardly any thing is to be found entire.

"Near to a vault, which is now thirty feet below ground, and has, probably, been a burial place, there is a draw-well, where there are several strata of *lavas, with earth to a considerable thickness over the surface of each stratum.* Recupero has made use of this as an argument to prove the great antiquity of the mountain. For if it require two thousand years or upward, to form but a scanty soil on the surface of a *lava,* there must have been more than that space of time betwixt each of the eruptions which have formed the strata. But what shall we say of a pit they sunk near to *Jaci* of a great depth. They pierced through *seven* distinct *lavas,* one under the other, the surfaces of which were parallel, and *most of them covered with a thick bed of rich earth.* Now, says he, the eruption which formed the lowest of these *lavas,* if we may be allowed to reason from analogy, must have flowed from the mountain at least fourteen thousand years ago."—*Vol. I. Letter* 7. Whereas the computation inferred, but without doubt inaccurately, from the Pentateuch, makes the earth itself only between five and six thousand years old.

the ocean must once have covered the country, at least as high up as Williamsburg.

Again, in digging several wells lately in this town, the teeth of sharks were found from sixty to ninety or a hundred feet below the surface of the earth. The probability is that these teeth were deposited by the shark itself; and as this fish is never known to infest very shallow streams, the conclusion is clear that this whole country has once been buried under several fathoms of water. At all events, these teeth must be considered as ascertaining what was once the surface of the earth here; which surface is very little higher than that of James river. Now if it be considered that there has been no perceptible difference wrought in the figure or elevation of the coast, nor, consequently, in the precipitation of the interior streams since the earliest recorded discovery of Virginia, which was two hundred years ago, it will follow, that James river must, for many hundreds, perhaps thousands of years, have been running, at least here, with a very rapid, headlong current; the friction whereof must certainly have rendered the channel much deeper than it was at the time of the deposition of these teeth. The result is clear, that the surface of the stream, which even now, after all this friction and consequent depression, is so nearly on a level with the site of the shark's teeth, must, originally, have been much higher. I take this to be an irrefragable proof, that the land here was then inundated; and as there is no ground between this and the Atlantic, higher than that on which Richmond is built, it seems to me indisputably certain, that the whole of this beautiful country was once covered with a dreary waste of water.*

* An elegant and well informed writer on the theory of the earth, under the signature of "An Inquirer," whose remarks were suggested by the perusal of this letter of the British Spy, observes that sea shells and other marine substances are found in every explored part of the world, "on the loftiest mountains of Europe and the still loftier Andes of South America." As the British Spy was not writing a regular and elaborate treatise on the origin of the earth, he did not deem it material to congregate all the facts which have been seen, and supposed, in relation to this subject.

Whether the British Spy is to be considered as an Englishman of rank on a tour through America, and writing the above letter in Richmond to his friend in London; or whether he is to be considered as one of our own citizens disposed to entertain the people of Richmond and its vicinity with a light and amusing speculation on the origin of their country, in either instance it was both more natural, and more interesting that the speculation should appear to have grown out of recent facts discovered in their own town or neighbourhood, and with which they are all supposed to be

To what curious and interesting reflections does this subject lead us? Over this hill on which I am now sitting and writing at my ease, and from which I look with delight on the landscape that smiles around me—over this hill and over this landscape, the billows of the ocean have rolled in wild and dreadful fury, while the leviathan, the whale and all the monsters of the deep, have disported themselves amid the fearful tempest.

Where was then the shore of the ocean? From this place, for eighty miles to the westward, the ascent of the country is very gradual; to and even up the Blue Ridge, marine shells and other phenomena are found, which demonstrate that *that* country too, has been visited by the ocean. How then has it emerged? Has it been by a sudden convulsion? Certainly not. No observing man, who has ever travelled from the Blue Ridge to the Atlantic, can doubt that this emersion has been effected by very slow gradations. For as you advance to the east, the proofs of the former submersion of the country thicken upon you. On

conversant, than on distant and controvertible facts, which it was not important to the inquiry, whether they knew or believed, or not.

the shores of York river, the bones of whales abound; and I have been not a little amused in walking on the sand beach of that river during the recess of the tide, and looking up at the high cliff or bank above me, to observe strata of sea shells not yet calcined, like those which lay on the beach under my feet, interspersed with strata of earth (the joint result, no doubt, of sand and putrid vegetables) exhibiting at once a sample of the manner in which the adjacent soil had been formed, and proof of the comparatively recent desertion of the waters.

Upon the whole, every thing here tends to confirm the ingenious theory of Mr. Buffon; that the eastern coasts of continents are enlarged by the perpetual revolution of the earth from west to east, which has the obvious tendency to conglomerate the loose sands of the sea on the eastern coast; while the tides of the ocean, drawn from east to west, against the revolving earth, contribute to aid the process, and hasten the alluvion. But admitting the Abbe Raynal's idea, that America is a far younger country than either of the other continents, or in other words, that America has emerged long since their formation, how did it happen that the materials, which compose this continent, were not accumu-

lated on the eastern coast of Asia? Was it that
the present mountains of America, then protuberances on the bed of the ocean, intercepted a
part of the passing sands which would otherwise
have been washed on the Asiatic shore, and thus
became the rudiments of this vast continent? If
so, America is under much greater obligations to
her barren mountains, than she has hitherto
supposed.

But while Mr. Buffon's theory accounts very
handsomely for the enlargement of the eastern
coast, it offers no kind of reason for any exten-
sion of the western; on the contrary, the very
causes assigned, to supply the addition to the
eastern, seem at first view to threaten a diminu-
tion of the western coast. Accordingly, Mr.
Buffon, we see, has adopted also the latter idea;
and, in the constant abluvion from the western
coast of one continent, has found a perennial
source of materials for the eastern coast of that
which lies behind it. This last idea, however,
by no means quadrates with the hypothesis, that
the mountains of America formed the original
stamina of the continent; for, on the latter supposition, the mountains themselves would constitute the western coast; since Mr. Buffon's theory
precludes the idea of any accession in that quar-

ter. But the mountains do not constitute the western coast. On the contrary, there is a wider extent of country between the great mountains in North America, and the Pacific or the northern oceans, than there is between the same mountains and the Atlantic ocean. Mr. Buffon's theory, therefore, however rational as to the eastern, becomes defective, as he presses it, in relation to the western coast; unless, to accommodate the theory, we suppose the total abrasion of some great mountain which originally constituted the western limit, and which was itself, the embryon of this continent. But for many reasons, and particularly the present contiguity to Asia, at one part, where such a mountain, according to the hypothesis, must have run, the idea of any such limit will be thought rather too extravagant for adoption. The fact is, that Mr. Buffon has considered his theory rather in its operation on a continent already established, than on the birth or primitive emersion of a continent from the ocean.

As to the western part of this continent, I mean that which lies beyond the Alleghany mountains, if it were not originally gained from the ocean, it has received an accumulation of earth by no means less wonderful. Far beyond

the Ohio, in piercing the earth for water, the
stumps of trees, bearing the most evident impressions of the axe, and on one of them the rust of
consumed iron, have been discovered between
ninety and a hundred feet below the present
surface of the earth. This is a proof, by the by,
not only that this immense depth of soil has
been accumulated in that quarter ; but that *that
new country*, as the inhabitants of the Atlantic
states call it, is, indeed, a very ancient one ; and
that North America has undergone more revolu-
tions in point of civilization, than have heretofore
been thought of, either by the European or
American philosophers. That part of this continent, which borders on the western ocean,
being almost entirely unknown, it is impossible
to say whether it exhibit the same evidence of
immersion which is found here. M'Kenzie,
however, the only traveller who has ever penetrated through this vast forest, records a curious
tradition among some of the western tribes of
Indians, to wit : that the world was once covered
with water. The tradition is embellished, as
usual with a number of very highly poetical fic-
tions. The fact, which I suppose to be couched
under it, is the ancient submersion of that part
of the continent. which certainly looks much

more like *a world* than the petty territory that was inundated by Eucalion's flood. If I remember aright, for I cannot immediately refer to the book, Stith, in his History of Virginia, has recorded a similar tradition among the Atlantic tribes of Indians. I have no doubt that if M'Kenzie had been as well qualified for scientific research, as he was undoubtedly honest, firm and persevering, it would have been in his power to have thrown great lights on this subject, as it relates to the western country.

For my own part, while I believe the present mountains of America to have constituted the original *stamina* of the continent, I believe at the same time, the western as well as the eastern country to be the effect of alluvion; produced too by the same causes: the rotation of the earth, and the planetary attraction of the ocean.

The perception of this will be easy and simple, if, instead of confounding the mind, by a wide view of the whole continent as it now stands, we carry back our imaginations to the time of its birth, and suppose some one of the highest pinnacles of the Blue Ridge to have just emerged above the surface of the sea. Now whether the rolling of the earth to the east give to the ocean, which floats loosely upon its bosom, an actual

counter-current, to the west,* which is occasionally further accelerated by the motion of the
tides in that direction, or whether this be not the

---

* This idea, which is merely stated *hypothetically*, is considered, by the Inquirer, as having been a position *absolutely*
taken by the British Spy: and as the reverse principle, (to
wit, that the motion of the waters is taken from and corres-
ponds with that of the solid earth,) *is so well established*, he
concludes that it must have been contested by the British
Spy through mere inadvertence. But, for my part, I do not
perceive how this hypothetical idea of the British Spy is, at
all, in collision with the doctrine of the diurnal or annual
revolution of the terraqueous globe.

The British Spy could not have been guilty of so great an
absurdity as to intend that the waters of the ocean deserted
their bed and broke over the eastern coasts and lofty mountains of opposing continents, in order to maintain their actual
counter-current to the west. It must have been clear to him,
that the ocean, keeping its bed, must attend the motion of the
earth, " not only on its axis, but in its orbit." But the question here is not as to the position of the whole ocean as it
relates to the whole earth; the question is merely as to the loco-
motion of the particles of the ocean, among themselves. For
although the ocean, as well as the solid earth, must perform a
complete revolution around their common axis once in twenty-
four hours, it does not follow, as I take it, that the globules
of the fluid ocean must, all this time, remain as fixed as the
atoms of the solid earth: they certainly may and certainly
have, from some cause or other, a subordinate motion among
themselves, frequently adverse to the general motion of the
globe; to wit, a current to the west. The atmosphere belongs
as much to this globe as the waters of the ocean do: that is

case ; still to our newly emerged pinnacle, which is whirled, by the earth's motion, through the waters of the deep, the consequences will be the

---

to say, it cannot any more than the ocean fly off and attach itself to any other planet. It feels, like the ocean, the gravitating power of the earth and the attraction of the neighbouring planets. It is affected, no doubt, very sensibly (at least the lower region of it) by the earth's diurnal rotation, and like the ocean, is compelled to attend her in her annual journey around the sun. But what of this? Does the atmosphere remain fixed in such a manner, as that the part of it, which our antipodes are respiring at this moment, is to furnish our diet, our *pabulum vitæ*, twelve hours hence? Certainly not; the atoms which compose the atmosphere are, we know, in spite of the earth's diurnal and annual motion, agitated and impelled in every direction; and so also, we equally well know, are the waters of the ocean.

If the Inquirer, when he says that "the motion of the earth is communicated to every part of it, whether solid or fluid," intend that the motion of the loose and fluid particles of the ocean take, from the earth, a flux among themselves to the east, the result would be an actual current to the east; which is not pretended. If he mean, that the globules of the ocean, unaffected by any other cause than the motion of the earth, would always maintain the same position in relation to each other, he may, indeed, allege a principle which is well established; but as it does not meet the approbation of my reason, and as I am not in the habit of reading merely that I may understand and believe, I must beg permission to enter my dissent to the principle. It would be difficult, if not impossible, so close as we are in the neighbourhood of the earth's attraction, to invent any apparatus by which a same as if there were this actual and strong current. For while the waters will be continually accumulated on the eastern coast of this pinna-

---

decisive experiment could be made on this subject. But, by the way of illustration, let us suppose the earth at rest; let us suppose the atmosphere, by the hand of the great Chymist who raised it into its present aeriform state, once more reduced to a fluid; let us suppose it, like a great ocean, to surround the earth within the torrid zone, (partitioned at right angles, by two or three mountains running from north to to south) and all its parts reposing in a halcyon calm : let us then suppose the earth whirled on its axis to the east, what would be the probable effect ? it is clear that the lower region of this superincumbent ocean would be most strongly bound by the earth's attraction; it is equally clear that the stratum of globules, immediately in contact with the earth, would adhere more strongly thereto, than to the fluid stratum which rested upon it; while this adhesion to the surface of the earth would be assisted by the many rugged protuberances on that surface. Hence the first motion of the earth, the lowest part of this circumambient ocean, being most powerfully attracted and attached to the earth, would slide under the fluid mass above it, and thereby produce an inequality in the upper surface of the water itself; an elevation in the eastern, a concavity in the western side of each partition; while the waters, from their tendency to seek their level, would strive to restore the balance, by falling constantly from east to west.

Whether this effect would continue for ever, or how long it would continue in our oceans as they are at present arranged, it is not easy to solve. But that a current from the east to the west would be at first produced, is as evident as the light of

cle, it is obvious that on the western coast,
(protected, as it would be, from the current, by
the newly risen earth,) the waters will always be

---

heaven; if it be denied, I demand the solution of the following phenomenon: if a plate be filled with oil or other fluid,
and the plate be then drawn in any direction, how does it
happen that the fluid will manifest a tendency to flow in the
opposite direction; insomuch that if the draught of the plate
be sudden, the fluid, running rapidly over the adverse edge
of the plate, shall discharge itself completely; leaving little
behind but the inferior stratum? I take it, that the man
who solves this phenomenon, satisfactorily, will be compelled
to resort to principles, which, when applied to our oceans,
resting loosely as they do on the earth which rolls under
them, would inevitably produce a western current; and this
current once produced it will be difficult to say why and when
it should cease. A current thus produced would be unequal
from the nature of its cause, at various depths: it would be
subject to temporary affections and alterations near its surface, by the winds, the tides and the diversified shapes of the
coasts on which the ocean rolls. The general tendency,
however, of the great mass of the waters would be to the
west.

I see no sound reason in renouncing Mr. Buffon's theory
either on account of the eloquent and beautiful manner in
which it is explained; nor because it has long had its just
portion of admirers; nor because there are other more modern theories. While we are children, it may be well enough
to lie passively on our backs and permit others to prepare and
feed us with the pap of science; but when our own judgments
and understandings have gained their maturity, it behoves
us, instead of being "a feather for every wind that blows,"

comparatively low and calm. The result is clear. The sands, borne along by the ocean's current over the northern and southern extremities of this pinnacle, will always have a tendency to settle in the calm behind it; and thus, by

---

instead of floating impotently before the *capricious current* of fashion and opinion, to heave out all our anchors; to take a position from which nothing shall move us but reason and truth, not novelty and fashion. In the progress of science, many principles, in my opinion, have been dropped to make way for others, which are newer but less true. And among them Mr. Buffon's theory of the earth. The effect of alluvion is so slow, that any one generation is almost unable to perceive the change wrought by it; hence, many people, unable to sit down and reflect on the wonders which time can do, fly off with a kind of puerile impatience, and resort to any thing, even a *bouleversemente* of a whole continent, rather than to depend on so slow and imperceptible an operation as that of alluvion. This is not philosophical. Neither on the other hand would it be philosophical to reject a theory because it might be new and unsupported by a name. On the contrary, the man who, on any branch of philosophy starts a new hypothesis, which has even the guise of reason, confers a benefit on the world; for he enlarges the ground of thought, and although not immediately in the temple of truth himself, may have dropped a hint, an accidental clew, which may serve to lead others to the door of the temple. In this spirit, I not only excuse, but am grateful even for the wildest of Dr. Darwin's philosophical chimeras. In the same spirit, I offer, without the expectation of its final adoption, the idea suggested by this note as to the cause of a western current.

perpetual accumulations, form a western coast, more rapidly perhaps than an eastern one; as we may see in miniature, by the capes and shallows collected by the still water, on each side, at the mouths of creeks, or below rocks, in the rapids of a river.

After this new-born point of earth had gained some degree of elevation, it is probable that successive coats of vegetation, according to Dr. Darwin's idea, springing up, then falling and dying on the earth, paid an annual tribute to the infant continent, while each rain which fell upon it, bore down a part of its substance and assisted perpetually in the enlargement of its area.

It is curious that the arrangement of the mountains both in North and South America, as well as the shape of the two continents, combine to strengthen the preceding theory. For the mountains, as you will perceive on inspecting your maps, run in chains from north to south; thus opposing the widest possible barrier to the sands, as they roll from east to west. The shape of the continent is just that which would naturally be expected from such an origin: that is, they lie along, collaterally, with the mountains. As far north as the country is well known, these ranges of mountains are observed; and it is remarkable, that as soon as the Cordilleras terminate in the south, the continent of South America ends: where they terminate in the north, the continent dwindles to a narrow isthmus.

Assuming this theory as correct, it is amusing to observe the conclusions to which it will lead us.

As the country is supposed to have been formed by gradual accumulations, and as these accumulations were most probably equal or nearly so in every part, it follows that, broken as this country is in hills and dales, it has assumed no new appearance by its emersion; but that the figure of the earth's surface is the same throughout, as well where it is now covered by the waters of the ocean as where it has been already denudated. So that Mr. Boyle's mountains in the sea, cease to have any thing wonderful in them.

Connected with this, it is not an improbable conclusion, that new continents and islands are now forming on the bed of the ocean. Perhaps, at some future day, lands may emerge in the neighbourhood of the Antarctic circle, which by progressive accumulations and a consequent increase of weight, may keep a juster balance

between the poles, and produce a material difference in our astronomical relations. The navigators of that day will be as successful in their
discoveries in the southern seas, as Columbus
was heretofore in the northern. For there can
be little doubt that there has been a time when
Columbus, if he had lived, would have found
his reasonings, on the balance of the earth,
fallacious; and would have sought these seas for
a continent, as much in vain, as Drake, Anson,
Cook and others, encouraged perhaps by similar
reasoning, have since sought the ocean of the
south.

If Mr. Buffon's notion be correct, that the
eastern coast of one continent is perpetually
feeding on the western coast of that which lies
before it, the conclusion is inevitable, that the
present materials of Europe and Africa, and Asia,
in succession, will at some future day, compose
the continents of North and South America;
while the latter, thrown on the Asiatic shore,
will again make a part, and, in time, the whole
of that continent, to which by some philosophers, they are supposed to have been originally
attached. It is equally clear that, by this means,
the continents will not only exchange their materials, but their position; so that, in process of

time, they must respectively make a tour around the globe, maintaining still the same ceremonious distance from each other, which they now hold.

According to my theory, which supposes an alluvion on the western as well as the eastern coast, the continents and islands of the earth, will be caused, reciprocally, to approximate, and (if materials enough can be found in the bed of the ocean, or generated by any process of nature) ultimately to unite. Our island of Great Britain, therefore, at some future day, and in proper person, will probably invade the territory of France. In the course of this work of alluvion, as it relates to this country, the refulgent waters of the Atlantic will be forced to recede from Hampton Roads and the Chesapeake; the beds whereof will become fertile valleys, or, as they are called here, river bottoms; while the lands in the lower district of the state, which are now only a very few feet above the surface of the sea, will rise into majestic eminences, and the present sickly site of Norfolk be converted into a high and salubrious mountain. I apprehend, however, that the present inhabitants of Norfolk would be extremely unwilling to have such an effect wrought in their day; since there can be little doubt that they prefer their present commercial situation, incumbered as it is by the annual visits of the yellow fever, to the elevation and health of the Blue Ridge.

In the course of this process, too, of which I have been speaking, if the theory be correct, the gulf of Mexico will be eventually filled up, and the West India islands consolidated with the American continent.

These consequences, visionary as they may now appear, are not only probable, but, if the alluvion which is demonstrated to have taken place already, should continue, they are inevitable. There is very little probability that the isthmus of Darien, which connects the two continents, is coeval with the Blue Ridge or the Cordilleras; and it requires only a continuation of the cause which produced the isthmus, to effect the repletion of the gulf and the consolidation of the islands with the continent.

But when? I am possessed of no *data* whereby the calculations can be made. The depth at which *Herculaneum* and *Pompeia* were found to be buried in the course of sixteen hundred years, affords us no light on this inquiry; because their burial was effected not by the slow alluvion and accumulation of time, but by the sudden

and repeated eruptions of Vesuvius. As little
are we aided by the repletion of the earth around
the *Tarpein* rock in *Rome;* since that repletion was most probably effected in a very great
degree, by the materials of fallen buildings. And
besides, the original height of the rock is not
ascertained with any kind of precision ; historians having, I believe, merely informed us, that
it was sufficiently elevated to kill the criminals
who were thrown from its summit.

But a truce with philosophy. Who could have
believed that the skeleton of an unwieldy whale,
and a few mouldering teeth of a shark, would
have led me such a dance !

Adieu, my dear S . . . . , for the present.
May the light of heaven continue to shine around
you !

LETTER III.

Richmond, September 15.

You inquire into the state of your favourite art in Virginia. Eloquence, My dear S. . . . ., has few successful votaries here: I mean eloquence of the highest order; such as that to which, not only the bosom of your friend, but the feelings of the whole British nation bore evidence, in listening to the charge of the Begums in the prosecution of Warren Hastings.

In the national and state legislatures, as well as at the various bars in the United States, I have heard great volubility, much good sense, and some random touches of the pathetic; but in the same bodies, I have heard a far greater proportion of puerile rant, or tedious and disgusting inanity. Three remarks are true as to almost all their orators.

First, They have not a sufficient fund of general knowledge.

Secondly, They have not the habit of close and solid thinking.

Thirdly, They do not aspire at original ornaments.

From these three defects, it most generally results, that although they pour out, easily enough, a torrent of words, yet these are destitute of the light of erudition, the practical utility of just and copious thought, or those novel and beautiful allusions and embellishments, with which the very scenery of the country is so highly calculated to inspire them.

The truth is, my dear S . . . , that this scarcity of genuine and sublime eloquence, is not confined to the United States : instances of it in any civilized country have always been rare indeed.   Mr. Blair is certainly correct in the opinion, that a state of nature is most favourable to the higher efforts of the imagination, and the more unrestrained and noble raptures of the heart.   Civilization, wherever it has gained ground, has interwoven with society a habit of artificial and elaborate decorum, which mixes in every operation of life, deters the fancy from every bold enterprise, and buries nature under a load of hypocritical ceremonies.   A man, therefore, in order to be eloquent, has to forget the habits in which he has been educated ; and never will he touch his audience so exquisitely as when he

goes back to the primitive simplicity of the patriarchal age.

I have said that instances of genuine and
sublime eloquence have always been rare in
every civilized country. It is true that Tully
and Pliny the younger have, in their epistles,
represented Rome, in their respective days, as
swarming with orators of the first class; yet
from the specimens which they themselves have
left us, I am led to entertain a very humble opinion of ancient eloquence.

Demosthenes we know has pronounced, not
the chief, but the sole merit of an orator to consist in *delivery*, or as Lord Verulam translates
it, in *action*, and, although I know that the
world would proscribe it as a literary heresy, I
cannot help believing Tully's merit to have been
principally of that kind. For my own part, I
confess very frankly, that I have never met with
any thing of his, which has, according to my
taste, deserved the name of superior eloquence.
His style, indeed, is pure, polished, sparkling,
full and sonorous ; and perhaps deserves all the
encomiums which have been bestowed on it.
But an oration, certainly, no more deserves the
title of superior eloquence, because its style is
ornamented, than the figure of an Apollo would

deserve the epithet of elegant, merely from the
superior texture and flow of the drapery. In
reading an oration, it is the mind to which I
look. It is the expanse and richness of the conception itself, which I regard, and not the glittering tinsel wherein it may be attired. Tully's
orations, examined in this spirit, have, with me,
sunk far below the grade at which we have
been taught to fix them.

It is true, that at school, I learned, like the
rest of the world, to lisp, "Cicero the orator:"
but when I grew up and began to judge for
myself, I opened his volumes again and looked
in vain for that sublimity of conception, which
fills and astonishes the mind ; that simple pathos
which finds such a sweet welcome in every
breast ; or that resistless enthusiasm of unaffected
passion, which takes the heart by storm. On
the contrary, let me confess to you that, whatever may be the cause, to me he seemed cold
and vapid, and uninteresting and tiresome : not
only destitute of that compulsive energy of thought
which we look for in a great man, but even void
of the strong, rich and varied colouring of a superior fancy. His masterpiece of composition, his
work, De Oratore, is, in my judgment, extremely
light and unsubstantial ; and in truth is little

more than a tissue of rhapsodies, assailing the ear indeed with pleasant sounds, but leaving few clear and useful traces on the mind.   Plutarch speaks of his person as all grace, his voice as perfect music, his look and gesture as all alive, striking, dignified and peculiarly impressive; and I incline to the opinion, that to these theatrical advantages, connected with the just reliance which the Romans had in his patriotism and good judgment, their strong interest in the subjects discussed by him, and their more intimate acquaintance with the idiom of his language, his fame while living, arose ; and that it has been since propagated by the schools on account of the classic purity and elegance of his style.

Many of these remarks are, in my opinion, equally applicable to Demosthenes.   He deserves, indeed, the distinction of having more fire and less smoke than Tully.   But in the majestic march of the mind, in the force of thought, and splendour of imagery, I think, both the orators of Greece and Rome eclipsed by more than one person within his majesty's dominions.

Heavens ! how should I be anathematized and excommunicated by every pedagogue in Great Britain, if these remarks were made public ! Spirits of Car and of Ascham ! have mercy upon me! Wo betide the hand that plucks the wizard beard of hoary error! From lisping infancy to stooping age, the reproaches, the curses of the world shall be upon it! But to you, my dearest S . . . . ., my friend, my preceptor, to you I disclose my opinions with the same freedom, and for the same purpose, that I would expose my wounds to a surgeon. To you, it is peculiarly proper that I should make my appeal on this subject; for when eloquence is the theme, your name is not far off.

Tell me then, you, who are capable of doing it, what is this divine eloquence. What the charm by which the orator binds the senses of his audience; by which he attunes and touches and sweeps the human lyre, with the resistless sway and master hand of a Timotheus? Is not the whole mystery comprehended in one word, SYMPATHY? I mean not merely that tender passion which quavers the lip and fills the eye of the babe when he looks on the sorrows and tears of another; but that still more delicate and subtile quality by which we passively catch the very colours, momentum and strength of the mind, to whose operations we are attending; which converts every speaker, to whom we listen, into a *Procrustes*, and enables him, for the moment, to stretch or lop our faculties to fit the standard of his own mind.

This is a very curious subject. I am sometimes half inclined to adopt the notion stated by our great Bacon in his original and masterly treatise on the advancement of learning " Fascination," says he, " is the power and act of imagination intensive upon other bodies than the body of the imaginant; wherein the school of Paracelsus and the disciples of pretended natural magic have been so intemperate, as that they have exalted the power of the imagination to be much one with the power of miracle-working faith : others that draw nearer to probability, calling to their view the secret passages of things, and especially of the contagion that passeth from body to body, do conceive it should likewise be agreeable to nature, *that there should be some transmissions and operations from spirit to spirit, without the mediation of the senses ;* whence the conceits have grown, now almost made civil, of the mastering spirit, and the force of confidence, and the like." This notion is further explained in his Sylva Sylvarum, wherein he tells a story of an Egyptian soothsayer, who made Mark Anthony believe that his genius, which was otherwise brave and confi-

dent, was, in the presence of Octavianus Cæsar-
poor and cowardly : and therefore he advised
him to absent himself as much as he could, and
remove far from him. It turned out, however,
that this soothsayer was suborned by Cleopatra,
who wished Anthony's company in Egypt.

Yet, if there be not something of this secret
intercourse from spirit to spirit, how does it happen that one speaker shall gradually invade and
benumb all the faculties of my soul as if I were
handling a torpedo ; while another shall awaken
and arouse me, like the clangour of the martial
trumpet? How does it happen that the first shall
infuse his poor spirit into my system, lethargize
my native intellects and bring down my powers
exactly to the level of his own? or that the last
shall descend upon me like an angel of light,
breathe new energies into my frame, dilate my
soul with his own intelligence, exalt me into a
new and nobler region of thought, snatch me
from the earth at pleasure, and rap me to the
seventh heaven? And, what is still more wonderful, how does it happen that these different
effects endure so long after the agency of the
speaker has ceased? Insomuch, that if I sit
down to any intellectual exercise, after listening
to the first speaker, my performance shall be

unworthy even of me, and the num-fish visible
and tangible in every sentence; whereas, if I
enter on the same amusement, after having
attended to the last mentioned orator, I shall be
astonished at the elevation and vigour of my
own thoughts; and if I meet, accidentally, with
the same production, a month or two afterward,
when my mind has lost the inspiration, shall
scarcely recognise it for my own work.

Whence is all this? To me it would seem
that it must proceed either from the subtile commerce between the spirits of men, which Lord
Verulam notices, and which enables the speaker
thereby to identify his hearer with himself; or
else that the mind of man possesses, independ-
ently of any volition on the part of its proprietor, a species of pupillary faculty of dilating and
contracting itself, in proportion to the pencil of
the rays of light which the speaker throws upon
it; which dilatation or contraction, as in the case
of the eye, cannot be immediately and abruptly
altered.

Whatever may be the solution, the fact, I
think, is certainly as I have stated it. And it is
remarkable that the same effect is produced,
though perhaps in a less degree, by perusing
books into which different degrees of spirit and

genius have been infused. I am acquainted with a gentlemen who never sits down to a composition, wherein he wishes to shine, without previously reading, with intense application, half a dozen pages of his favourite Bolingbroke. Having taken the character and impulse of that writer's mind, he declares that he feels his pen to flow with a spirit not his own; and that, if, in the course of his work, his powers begin to languish, he finds it easy to revive and charge them afresh from the same never-failing source.

If these things be not visionary, it becomes important to a man, for a new reason, what books he reads, and what company he keeps, since, according to Lord Verulam's notion, an influx of the spirits of others may change the native character of his heart and understanding, before he is aware of it; or, according to the other suggestion, he may so habitually contract the pupil of his mind, as to be disqualified for the comprehension of a great subject, and fit only for microscopic observations. Whereas by keeping the company and reading the works of men of magnanimity and genius only, he may receive their qualities by subtile transmission, and eventually, get the eye, the ardour and the enterprise of an eagle.

But whither am I wandering? Permit me to return. Admitting the correctness of the principles formerly mentioned, it would seem to be a fair conclusion that whenever an orator wishes to know what effect he has wrought on his audience, he should coolly and conscientiously propound to himself this question: Have I, myself, throughout my oration, felt those clear and cogent convictions of judgment, and that pure and exalted fire of the soul, with which I wished to inspire others? For, he may rely on it, that he can no more impart (or to use Bacon's word, transmit) convictions and sensations which he himself has not, at the time, sincerely felt, than he can convey a clear title to property, in which he himself has no title.

This leads me to remark a defect which I have noticed more than once in this country. Following up too closely the cold conceit of the Roman division of an oration, the speakers set aside a particular part of their discourse, usually the peroration, in which, they take it into their heads that they will be pathetic. Accordingly when they reach this part, whether it be prompted by the feelings or not, a mighty bustle commences. The speaker pricks up his ears, erects his chest, tosses his arms with hysterical vehemence, and says every thing which he supposes ought to affect his hearers; but it is all in vain; for it is obvious that every thing he says is prompted by the head; and, however it may display his ingenuity and fertility, however it may appeal to the admiration of his hearers, it will never strike deeper. The *hearts* of the audience will refuse all commerce except with the *heart* of the speaker; nor, in this commerce is it possible, by any disguise, however artful, to impose false ware on them. However the speaker may labour to seem to feel, however near he may approach to the appearance of the reality, the heart nevertheless possesses a keen unerring sense, which never fails to detect the imposture. It would seem as if the heart of man stamps a secret mark on all its effusions, which alone can give them currency, and which no ingenuity, however adroit, can successfully counterfeit.

I have been not a little diverted, here, in listening to some fine orators, who deal almost entirely in this pathos of the head. They practise the start, the pause—make an immense parade of attitudes and gestures, and seem to imagine themselves piercing the heart with a thousand wounds. The heart all the time, developing every trick that is played to cajole her, and sitting serene and composed, looks on and smiles at the ridiculous pageant as it passes.

Nothing can, in my opinion, be more ill-judged in an orator, than to indulge himself in this idle, artificial parade. It is particularly unfortunate in an exordium. It is as much as to say *caveat auditor;* and for my own part, the moment I see an orator rise with this menacing majesty; assume a look of solemn wisdom; stretch forth his right arm, like the *rubens dexter* of Jove; and hear him open his throat in deep and tragic tone; I feel myself involuntarily braced, and in an attitude of defence, as if I were going to take a bout with Mendoza.

The Virginians boast of an orator of nature, whose manner was the reverse of all this; and he is the only orator of whom they do boast, with much emphasis. I mean the celebrated Patrick Henry, whom I regret that I came to this country too late to see. I cannot, indeed, easily forgive him, even in the grave, his personal instrumentality in separating these fair colonies from Great Britain. Yet I dare not withhold from the memory of his talents, the tribute of respect to which they are so justly entitled.

I am told that his general appearance and manners were those of a plain farmer or planter

of the back country; that, in this character, he
always entered on the exordium of an oration; disqualifying himself, with looks and
expressions of humility so lowly and unassuming, as threw every heart off its guard and
induced his audience to listen to him, with the
same easy openness with which they would converse with an honest neighbour : but, by and by,
when it was little expected, he would take a
flight so high, and blaze with a splendour so
heavenly, as filled them with a kind of religious
awe, and gave him the force and authority of a
prophet.

You remember this was the manner of Ulysses ; commencing with the look depressed and
hesitating voice.   Yet I dare say Mr. Henry was
directed to it, not by the example of Ulysses, of
which it is very probable, that, at the commence-
ment of his career, at least, he was entirely ignorant : but either that it was the genuine,
trembling diffidence, without which, if Tully
may be believed, a great orator never rises ; or
else that he was prompted to it by his own sound
judgment and his intimate knowledge of the
human heart.

I have seen the skeletons of some of his orations.   The periods and their members are short,

quick, eager, palpitating, and are manifestly the extemporaneous effusions of a mind deeply convinced, and a heart inflamed with zeal for the propagation of those convictions. They afford, however, a very inadequate sample of his talents: the stenographer having never attempted to follow him, when he arose in the strength and awful majesty of his genius.

I am not a little surprised to find eloquence of this high order so negligently cultivated in the United States. Considering what a very powerful engine it is in a republic, and how peculiarly favourable to its culture the climate of republics has been always found, I expected to have seen in America more votaries to Mercury than even to Plutus. Indeed it would be so sure a road both to wealth and honours, that if I coveted either, and were an American, I would bend all my powers to its acquirement, and try whether I could not succeed as well as Demosthenes in vanquishing natural imperfections. Ah! my dear S . . . . , were you a citizen of this country! You, under the influence of whose voice a parliament of Great Britain has trembled and shuddered, while her refined and enlightened galleries have wept and fainted in the excess of feeling! what might you not accomplish? But, for the honour of my country, I am much better pleased that you are a Briton.

On the subject of Virginian eloquence, you shall hear further from me.   In the mean time adieu, my S . . . . , my friend, my father.

Sir,

As the theory of the earth derives importance from its dignity, if not from its utility, and has of late years given birth to many ingenious speculations, I shall offer no apology for troubling you with the following remarks, which were suggested by an essay, in last Wednesday's Argus, entitled "The British Spy."

Sea shells and other marine productions, differing in no respect from those which now exist in their native element, have been found in every explored part of the globe. They are found, too, in the highest as well as in the lowest situations: on the loftiest mountains of Europe, and the still loftier Andes of South America. To go no farther from home, our own Alleghany abounds with them. How were these substances separated from their parent ocean? Do they still remain in their primitive beds? and has the water deserted them? or have they deserted the water? These questions, differently answered, give rise to different theories.

Among these theories, that of the Count de Buffon stand conspicuous. Adorned with all the graces of style, and borrowing a lustre from his other splendid productions, it has long had its full share of admirers. After exhibiting new proofs of a former submersion, in which he discovers great ingenuity, and is certainly entitled to great praise, he proceeds to account for the earth in its present form, by a natural operation of the ocean which covered it. This hypothesis, which the British Spy has partially adopted, is liable to many objections, which, to me at least, are insuperable. I will briefly notice some of the most obvious.

Although alluvion may account for small accessions of soil nearly on a level with the ocean, it cannot explain the formation of mountains. It is contrary to all the known laws of nature to suppose that a fluid could lift, so far above its own level, bodies many times heavier than itself.

Again, if the ocean, as Buffon maintains, have a tendency to wear away all points and eminences over which it passes, it would exert this tendency on the mountains itself had formed ; or rather, it would prevent their formation. It is surely inconsistent to suppose the ocean would produce mountains, and at the same time wear away those that already existed. Indeed, the author himself seemed to be aware of the invincible objections to this part of his theory, and endeavours to evade their force by sinking a part of the earth, in the cavity occasioned by which, the superfluous waters find a sufficient receptacle; thus abandoning the agency of alluvion, and adopting a new and totally different hypothesis.

But while marine substances are found far *above* their proper element, vegetable bodies are often found far *below* the seat of their production. In Europe they often meet with wood, at great depths of the earth, in a state of perfect preservation; and in sinking wells, in this country, trunks of trees frequently obstruct the progress of the work. A Mr. Peters, of Harrison county, not long since, met with pieces of pine, twenty feet below the surface, on a hill of considerable elevation, and at a distance from any watercourse. In this town, leaves, believed to be those of the hazle, were found mingled with marine productions. These vegetable matters must have been once exposed to air, heat and light, to have attained the state in which they were found; and the same exposure would have afterwards caused their decay, unless their interment had been sudden and complete. Bones, shells and other extraneous substances, are often found bedded in marble and other hard bodies; and I myself have seen a specimen of those human bones, which in the fortifications of Gibraltar are often found incorporated with the solid rock. What less than some great throe of nature, or some mighty agent, now dormant and unknown, could have produced the general *bouleversement* which these appearances indicate?

But the hypothetical reasoning of Monsieur de Buffon is founded on a fact no less hypothetical. The arguments in favour of a general current to the west, are, I confess, very cogent, and would be convincing but for the following difficulties:

1. If the operation of the sun and moon, in producing alternate elevations and depressions of the ocean, produce also a current, the force of this current will be in proportion to the mass of water thus raised and depressed. Now, contrary to the assertion of Buffon, the tides are highest in high latitudes, and gradually diminish towards the equator, where I believe they hardly exceed a foot. By the observations of Captain Cook, the same difference exists in the Pacific ocean as was long known in the Atlantic. If then

there be a general current to the west, it should
be strongest in high latitudes and weakest under
the line. But the contrary is the fact. No
general current to the west is found without the
tropics ; and that which prevails irregularly
between them is usually and rationally ascribed
to the trade winds.

2. If this supposed current existed, its effect
would be readily perceived by our navigators in
the difference of their passages to and from Europe ; but, the one before referred to excepted,
they meet with nothing of the kind. A current,
at the rate of one mile an hour, would make a
difference of near two thousand miles between
an ordinary voyage to and from Europe.

3. By actual observations, detailed in the
second volume of the Philosophical Transactions,
the prevailing currents about some islands in the
Atlantic ocean are to the east. At Owhyhee,
which lies within the tropics, and nearly in the
middle of the Pacific ocean, Captain Cook observed the current to set, without any regularity,
sometimes to the west and sometimes to the east.

4. But one argument may be deemed conclusive. The air is a fluid at least as sensible to
the gravitating power of the planet as the ocean,
and like that, must also have its tides. If, on

the one hand, the tides of the air are more liable
to be disturbed by its compressibility, by partial
rarefaction or condensation, its obstacles, on the
other hand, to a free motion round the earth,
are comparatively inconsiderable. Its course is
somewhat impeded, but never arrested. If then
such a general law existed, as is contended for,
there would be, either a steady east wind, or
greater flow of air from that quarter than from
the west, in every climate of the globe. But
this is the case only between the tropics ; and
the prevalence of the east wind, in that region,
has been almost universally ascribed to rarefaction by heat, since no other solution can account
for the sea and land breezes, monsoons, and
other phenomena of those climates.

From these considerations I am disposed to
think, that there is no uniform current to the
west ; or that it is too inconsiderable to have any
effect on the figure of the earth. Admitting the
existence of a general current, it may be merely
superficial. Currents, whose force gradually
diminishes from the surface downwards, are
known to exist ; and the practice of seamen,
when they wish "to try the current," is evidently
founded on the belief that they do not extend to
great depths. The accession of water by the

tides is too small to require a general movement of the ocean to its bottom.

In weighing the probability of a general current to the west, I have confined myself to the operation of the tides ; as the mere motion of the earth, either in its orbit, or on its axis, can have no possible effect this way. This motion is communicated to every part of the earth, whether solid or fluid ; and while it continues equable, they are both affected alike, and their relative situations remain the same. So well established a principle must have been contested by the British Spy through mere inadvertence.

If, after all that has been said, arguments, in favour of a current from the surface to the bottom, be deemed conclusive, it is worth while to inquire into its probable effects.

The British Spy supposes that this general current enlarges both the eastern and western coasts of continents ; in which hypothesis, he differs less from Buffon than that elegant but fanciful theorist differs from himself. For, in his theory on the formation of the planets, he advances that the ocean is continually wearing away the eastern coasts, and by a process, which he does not even hint at, enlarging the western ; and that Asia is an older country than Europe.

But in a subsequent work, his Epochs, he maintains the direct reverse, and mentions the abruptness of the western, and the greater number of islands of the eastern coasts, as evidences that the former have been abraded by the ocean.

But I find neither reasoning nor fact to warrant either of these conclusions. It has been observed that a shore forms a convex outline where it gains on the ocean, and a concave where it loses. On inspecting the map of the world, we perceive nothing which by this standard indicates a greater increase on one continent than on the other, or even any increase at all. We see no vast prominence of coast under the line; but on taking both shores of the ocean, *in both hemispheres*, into comparison, we find that the convexities on the western side are balanced by equal convexities on the eastern. Besides it is clear that in proportion as the contents of the ocean are cast on the land, in the same degree it becomes deeper, and its shores more steep and abrupt. This is as true of the ocean as it is of a ditch. By this increasing declivity of growing shores, the additional gravity to be overcome will, in time, check the alluvion of any current, however strong. An opposite equalizing tendency occurs, where the coast is worn away by the ocean. Successive fragments of rocks and precipices, by sloping the shore, gradually abate the impetus of the waters, until the coast attains that due inclination by which the gravity to be overcome exactly counterbalances the projectile force of the ocean. Without doubt, small variations continually take place in the outline of all coasts ; but the equilibrium for which I contend, is founded on correct principles ; and every coast, whether eastern or western, approaches to that form, if it have not already attained it, when what it loses *by the ocean* will be precisely equal to what it gains.

It should be remarked that Buffon, in his last addition to his *Theorie*, conscious of the insufficiency of alluvion in the formation of continents, supposes that the cavities, with which the earth abounds, are continually falling in, and from the consequent retreat of the ocean, that continents are continually approximating. This conjecture certainly renders his theory more consistent ; but it substitutes a cause for the immersion of the earth totally different from his first hypothesis of alluvion : and it has been that alone which I have considered. This last supposition is merely gratuitous ; as neither observation nor history afford us any proofs of the existence of these immense caverns, or of any general retreat of the ocean.

For the reasons which I have given, and for many more, the theory of this celebrated naturalist has long been deemed both improbable and inadequate, and is now confined to the merit, (no small merit by the by,) of having collected valuable materials, and detected the fallacies of Burnet, Woodward and other dreamers on the subject. It has accordingly given place to new theories, more consistent at least, if not more satisfactory.

Volcanoes, and intense heat in the centre of the earth, the recrements of animals and vegetables, have been employed, as separate or joint agents, by the speculators on this curious subject. Dr. Hutton, by far the most celebrated of these, supposes the exuviæ of shell fish to have constituted the basis of the earth; and that it has assumed its present form and appearance by the fusion produced by the earth's internal heat. He supports this opinion by a train of elaborate reasoning, and a chemical examination of the bodies which compose the outer crust of the earth. I regret that I am acquainted with the work only at second hand. But I believe that even this theory, ingenious and scientific as it is, gives little more general satisfaction than those which preceded it. It is, in common with the other late hypothesis, opposed by the fine reasoning of Buffon, in favour of the immediate action of water in producing the correspondent angles of mountains, their waving outline, parallel strata, &c., as well as by many of the facts I have glanced at; and it is, moreover, said to be contradicted by some chemical experiments, at once pertinent and clear.

On the whole, then, I fear we have not yet arrived at that certainty which will satisfy the inquirer who is neither enamoured with the fancies of his own brain, nor seduced by the eloquence of others; and therefore, to use the words of an elegant writer of our own country, who discovers the same acuteness, the same philosophic caution on this as on other occasions, " we must be contented to acknowledge that this great phenomenon is, yet, unsolved. Ignorance is preferable to error; and he is less remote from the truth who believes nothing, than he who believes what is wrong."

Before we can obtain a sober conviction on the subject, or even properly compare the probability of the respective theories, many questions now contested must be settled; new facts must be discovered; new powers of nature developed.

How far does the power of aqueous solution and of crystallization extend? Does the earth borrow all its heat from the sun? or has it a perennial source in its own bowels? are there general currents in the ocean? if so, what are their courses, periods and strength? It is clear that every rain that falls, every wind that blows, transports some portion of the earth we inhabit to the ocean. Is there any secret and magical process in nature, as some have supposed, by which this perpetual waste is perpetually repaired? and do mountains receive accessions by rain, by attraction, or any other mode equal to what they evidently lose? Again, water is converted into vegetables, vegetables into animals, and both of these again into earth. Is this same earth reconverted into water, and by one unvaried round of mutation, each preserved in its present proportion to all eternity?

Science, with an ardour of inquiry never before known, and a daily increase of materials, advances with hasty steps to answer these pre-

liminary questions; but till they are solved I
incline to think that every theory is premature
and shall, therefore, remain satisfied with the
safe, but humble character of

AN INQUIRER.

LETTER IV.

Richmond, September 22.

I HAVE just returned, my dear S . . . . ., from an interesting morning's ride. My object was to visit the site of the Indian town, Powhatan ; which you will remember was the metropolis of the dominions of Pocahuntas's father, and, very probably, the birth-place of that celebrated princess.

The town was built on the river, about two miles below the ground now occupied by Richmond; that is, about two miles below the head of tide water. The land whereon it stood is, at present, part of a beautiful and valuable farm belonging to a gentleman by the name of William Mayo.

Aware of the slight manner in which the Indians have always constructed their habitations, I was not at all disappointed in finding no vestige of the old town. But as I traversed the ground over which Pocahuntas had so often bounded and frolicked in the sprightly morning of her youth, I could not help recalling the principal features of her history, and heaving a sigh of mingled pity and veneration to her memory.

Good Heaven! What an eventful life was hers! To speak of nothing else, the arrival of the English in her father's dominions must have appeared (as indeed it turned out to be) a most portentous phenomenon. It is not easy for us to conceive the amazement and consternation which must have filled her mind and that of her nation at the first appearance of our countrymen. Their great ship, with all her sails spread, advancing in solemn majesty to the shore; their complexion; their dress; their language; their domestic animals; their cargo of new and glittering wealth; and then the thunder and irresistible force of their artillery; the distant country announced by them, far beyond the great water, of which the oldest Indian had never heard, or thought, or dreamed—all this was so new, so wonderful, so tremendous, that I do seriously suppose, the personal descent of an army of Milton's celestial angels, robed in light, sporting in the bright beams of the sun and redoubling their splendour, making divine harmony with their golden harps, or playing with the bolt and chasing the rapid lightning of heaven, would excite not more astonishment in Great Britain than did the debarkation of the English among the aborigines of Virginia.

Poor Indians! Where are they now? Indeed, my dear S......, this is a truly afflicting consideration. The people here may say what they please; but, on the principles of eternal truth and justice, they have no right to this country. They say that they have bought it— bought it! Yes;—of whom? Of the poor trembling natives who knew that refusal would be vain; and who strove to make a merit of necessity by seeming to yield with grace, what they knew that they had not the power to retain. Such a bargain might appease the conscience of a gentleman of the green bag, "worn and hackneyed" in the arts and frauds of his profession; but in heaven's chancery, my S......, there can be little doubt that it has been long since set aside on the ground of duress.

Poor wretches! No wonder that they are so implacably vindictive against the white people; no wonder that the rage of resentment is handed down from generation to generation; no wonder that they refuse to associate and mix permanently with their unjust and cruel invaders and exterminators; no wonder that in the unabating spite and frenzy of conscious impotence, they wage an eternal war, as well as they are able; that they triumph in the rare opportunity of revenge; that they dance, sing and rejoice, as the victim shrieks and faints amid the flames, when they imagine all the crimes of their oppressors collected on his head, and fancy the spirits of their injured forefathers hovering over the scene, smiling with ferocious delight at the grateful spectacle, and feasting on the precious odour as it arises from the burning blood of the white man.

Yet the people, here, affect to wonder that the Indians are so very unsusceptible of civilization; or, in other words, that they so obstinately refuse to adopt the manners of the white men. Go, Virginians; erase, from the Indian nation, the tradition of their wrongs; make them forget, if you can, that once this charming country was theirs; that over these fields and through these forests their beloved forefathers, once, in careless gaiety, pursued their sports and hunted their game; that every returning day found them the sole, the peaceful, the happy proprietors of this extensive and beautiful domain. Make them forget, too, if you can, that in the midst

of all this innocence, simplicity and bliss—the
white man came; and lo!—the animated chase,
the feast, the dance, the song of fearless, thought-
less joy were over ; that ever since, they have
been made to drink of the bitter cup of humilia-
tion; treated like dogs; their lives, their liberties,
the sport of the white men ; their country and
the graves of their fathers torn from them, in
cruel succession : until, driven from river to river,
from forest to forest, and through a period of two
hundred years, rolled back, nation upon nation,
they find themselves fugitives, vagrants and stran-
gers in their own country, and look forward to
the certain period when their descendants will
be totally extinguished by wars, driven at the
point of the bayonet into the western ocean, or
reduced to a fate still more deplorable and horrid,
the condition of slaves. Go, administer the cup
of oblivion to recollections and anticipations
like these, and then you will cease to complain
that the Indian refuses to be civilized. But
until then, surely it is nothing wonderful that a
nation even yet bleeding afresh, from the memory of ancient wrongs, perpetually agonized
by new outrages, and goaded into desperation
and madness at the prospect of the certain ruin
which awaits their descendants, should hate the

authors of their miseries, of their desolation, their destruction; should hate their manners, hate their colour, their language, their name, and every thing that belongs to them. No: never, until time shall wear out the history of their sorrows and their sufferings, will the Indian be brought to love the white man, and to imitate his manners.

Great God! To reflect, my S . . . ., that the authors of all these wrongs were our own countrymen, our forefathers, professors of the meek and benevolent religion of Jesus! Oh! it was impious; it was unmanly; poor and pitiful! Gracious heaven! what had these poor people done? The simple inhabitants of these peaceful plains, what wrong, what injury had they offered to the English? My soul melts with pity and shame.

As for the present inhabitants, it must be granted that they are comparatively innocent; unless indeed they also have encroached under the guise of treaties, which they themselves have previously contrived to render expedient or necessary to the Indians.

Whether this has been the case or not, I am too much a stranger to the interior transactions of this country to decide. But it seems to me that were I a president of the United States, I would glory in going to the Indians, throwing myself on my knees before them, and saying to them, "Indians, friends, brothers, O ! forgive my countrymen ! Deeply have our forefathers wronged you ; and they have forced us to continue the wrong. Reflect, brothers ; it was not our fault that we were born in your country ; but now we have no other home ; we have no where else to rest our feet. Will you not, then, permit us to remain ? Can you not forgive even us, innocent as we are ? If you can, O ! come to our bosoms ; be, indeed, our brothers ; and since there is room enough for us all, give us a home in your land, and let us be children of the same affectionate family." I believe that a magnanimity of sentiment like this, followed up by a correspondent greatness of conduct on the part of the people of the United States, would go further to bury the tomahawk and produce a fraternization with the Indians, than all the presents, treaties and missionaries that can be employed; dashed and defeated as these latter means always are, by a claim of rights on the part of the white people which the Indians know to be false and baseless. Let me not be told that the Indians are too dark and fierce to be affected by generous and noble sentiments. I will not believe it. Magnanimity can never be lost on a nation which has produced an Alknomok, a Logan, and a Pocahuntas.

The repetition of the name of this amiable princess brings me back to the point from which I digressed. I wonder that the Virginians, fond as they are of anniversaries, have instituted no festival or order in honour of her memory. For my own part, I have little doubt, from the histories which we have of the first attempts at colonizing their country, that Pocahuntas deserves to be considered as the patron deity of the enterprise. When it is remembered how long the colony struggled to get a footing; how often sickness or famine, neglect at home, mismanagement here, and the hostilities of the natives, brought it to the brink of ruin; through what a tedious lapse of time, it alternately languished and revived, sunk and rose, sometimes hanging like Addison's lamp, "quivering at a point," then suddenly shooting up into a sickly and short-lived flame; in one word, when we recollect how near and how often it verged towards total extinction, maugre the patronage of Pocahuntas; there is the strongest reason to believe that, but for her patronage, the anniversary cannon of the

Fourth of July would never have resounded throughout the United States.

Is it not probable, that this sensible and amiable woman, perceiving the superiority of the Europeans, foreseeing the probability of the subjugation of her countrymen, and anxious as well to soften their destiny, as to save the needless effusion of human blood, desired, by her marriage with Mr. Rolfe, to hasten the abolition of all distinction between Indians and white men; to bind their interests and affections by the nearest and most endearing ties, and to make them regard themselves as one people, the children of the same great family? If such were her wise and benevolent views, and I have no doubt but they were, how poorly were they backed by the British court? No wonder at the resentment and indignation with which she saw them neglected; no wonder at the bitterness of the disappointment and vexation which she expressed to captain Smith, in London, arising as well from the cold reception which she herself had met, as from the contemptuous and insulting point of view in which she found that her nation was regarded.

Unfortunate princess! She deserved a happier fate! But I am consoled by these reflec-

tions: first, that she sees her descendants among
the most respectable families in Virginia; and
that they are not only superior to the false shame
of disavowing her as their ancestor; but that
they pride themselves, and with reason too, on
the honour of their descent; secondly, that she
herself has gone to a country, where she finds
her noble wishes realized; where the distinction
of colour is no more; but where, indeed, it is
perfectly immaterial "what complexion an Indian or an African sun may have burned" on
the pilgrim.

Adieu, my dear S .... This train of thought
has destroyed the tone of my spirits; when I
recover them you shall hear further from me.
Once more, adieu.

LETTER V.*

Richmond, September 23.

THIS town, my dear S . . . . . , is the residence of several conspicuous characters ; some of whose names we have heard on the other side of the Atlantic. You shall be better acquainted with them before we finish this correspondence. For the present permit me to introduce to your acquaintance, the . . . . . of the commonwealth of Virginia, and the . . . . of the United States.

These gentlemen are eminent political opponents ; the first belonging to the republican, the latter leading the van of the federal, party. Such is the interest which they both have in the confidence and affections of their respective parties, that it would be difficult, if not impos-

---

* The donee of the manuscript begs that he may not be considered as responsible for the accuracy with which certain characters are delineated in this letter. He selects it purely for the advantage which, he supposes, youthful readers may derive from the writer's reflections on the characters attempted to be drawn by him.

sible, for any Virginian to delineate either of their characters justly. Friendship or hostility would be almost sure to overcharge the picture. But for me, I have so little connexion with this country, or her concerns, either at present or in prospect, that I believe I can look on her most exalted characters without envy or prejudice of any kind; and draw them with the same cool and philosophic impartiality, as if I were a sojourner from another planet. If I fail in the delineation, the fault must be in the hand or in the head, in the pencil or the judgment: and not in any prepossession near my heart.

I choose to bring those two characters before you, together; because they exhibit, with great vivacity, an intellectual *phenomenon*, which I have noticed more than once before; and in the solution of which I should be pleased to see your pen employed: I mean the very different celerity in the movement of two sound minds, which on all subjects, wherein there is no mixture of party zeal, will ultimately come to the same just conclusion. What a pity it is, that Mr. Locke, while he was dissecting the human understanding, with such skill and felicity, did not advert to this characteristic variance in the minds of men. It would have been in his power, by de-

veloping its causes either to point to the remedy
if it exist at all, or to relieve the man of slow
mind, from the labour of fruitless experiments,
by showing the total impracticability of his cure.
But, to our gentlemen; and in order that you
may know them the more intimately, I will endeavour to prefix to each character a portrait of
the person.

The .... of this commonwealth is the
same ...... who was, not many years ago, the
.... at Paris. His present office is sufficient evidence of the estimation in which he is
held by his native state. In his stature, he is
about the middle height of men, rather firmly
set, with nothing further remarkable in his person, except his muscular compactness and apparent ability to endure labour. His countenance,
when grave, has rather the expression of stern-
ness and irascibility; a smile however, (and a
smile is not unusual with him in a social circle,)
lights it up to very high advantage, and gives it
a most impressive and engaging air of suavity
and benevolence. Judging merely from his
countenance, he is between the ages of forty-five
and fifty years. His dress and personal appearance are those of a plain and modest gentleman.
He is a man of soft, polite and even assiduous

attentions; but these, although they are always well-timed, judicious, and evidently the offspring of an obliging and philanthropic temper, are never performed with the striking and captivating graces of a Marlborough or a Bolingbroke. To be plain, there is often in his manner an inartificial and even an awkward simplicity, which while it provokes the smile of a more polished person, forces him to the opinion that Mr. . . . . . is a man of a most sincere and artless soul.

Nature has given him a mind neither rapid nor rich; and therefore, he cannot shine on a subject which is entirely new to him. But to compensate him for this, he is endued with a spirit of generous and restless emulation, a judgment solid, strong and clear, and a habit of application, which no difficulties can shake; no labours can tire.

With these aids simply, he has qualified himself for the first honours of this country; and presents a most happy illustration of the truth of the maxim, *Quisque, suæ fortunæ, faber*. For his emulation has urged him to perpetual and unremitting inquiry; his patient and unwearied industry has concentrated before him all the lights which others have thrown on the subjects of his consideration, together with all those which his own mind, by repeated efforts, is enabled to strike; while his sober, steady and faithful judgment has saved him from the common error of more quick and brilliant geniuses; the too hasty adoption of specious, but false conclusions.

These qualities render him a safe and an able counsellor. And by their constant exertion, he has amassed a store of knowledge, which, having passed seven times through the crucible, is almost as highly corrected as human knowledge can be; and which certainly may be much more safely relied on than the spontaneous and luxuriant growth of a more fertile, but less chastened mind—" a wild, where weeds and flowers promiscuous shoot."

Having engaged very early, first in the life of a soldier, then of a statesman, then of a laborious practitioner of the law, and finally, again of a politician, his intellectual operations have been almost entirely confined to juridical and political topics. Indeed, it is easy to perceive, that the mind of a man, engaged in so active a life must possess more native suppleness, versatility and vigour, than that of Mr. . . . . . , to be able to make an advantageous tour of the sciences in the rare interval of importunate duties. It is possible that the early habit of contemplating

subjects as expanded as the earth itself, with all
the relative interests of the great nations thereof,
may have inspired him with an indifference,
perhaps an inaptitude, for mere points of literature.   Algernon Sidney has said that he deems
all studies unworthy the serious regard of a man,
except the study of the principles of just government; and Mr. . . . . , perhaps, concurs with
our countryman in this as well as in his other
principles.   Whatever may have been the occasion, his acquaintance with the fine arts is certainly very limited and superficial; but, making
allowances for his bias towards republicanism, he
is a profound and even an eloquent statesmen.

Knowing him to be attached to that political
party, who, by their opponents, are 'called sometimes democrats, sometimes jacobins; and aware
also, that he was a man of warm and even ardent temper, I dreaded much, when I first
entered his company, that I should have been
shocked and disgusted with the narrow, virulent
and rancorous invectives of party animosity.*
How agreeably, how delightfully, was I disappointed!   Not one sentiment of intolerance pol-
luted his lips.   On the contrary, whether they

---

* The cloven foot of the Briton is visible; or, else, why from
the premises could he have expected such a consequence?

be the offspring of rational induction, of the habit of surveying men and things on a great scale, of native magnanimity, or of a combination of all those causes, his principles, as far as they were exhibited to me, were forbearing, liberal, widely extended and great.

As the elevated ground, which he already holds, has been gained merely by the dint of application; as every new step which he mounts becomes a mean of increasing his powers still further, by opening a wider horizon to his view, and thus stimulating his enterprise afresh, reinvigorating his habits, multiplying the materials and extending the range of his knowledge; it would be matter of no surprise to me, if, before his death, the world should see him at the head of the American administration. So much for the . . . . of the commonwealth of Virginia : a living, an honourable, an illustrious monument of self-created eminence, worth and greatness !

Let us now change the scene and lead forward a very different character indeed : a truant, but a highly favoured pupil of nature. It would seem as if this capricious goddess had finished the two characters, purely with the view of exhibiting a vivid contrast. Nor is this contrast confined to their minds.

The . . . . of the United States is, in his person, tall, meager, emaciated ; his muscles relaxed, and his joints so loosely connected, as not only to disqualify him, apparently, for any vigorous exertion of body, but to destroy every thing like elegance and harmony in his air and movements. Indeed, in his whole appearance, and demeanour ; dress, attitudes, gesture ; sitting, standing or walking ; he is as far removed from the idolized graces of lord Chesterfield, as any other gentleman on earth. To continue the portrait : his head and face are small in proportion to his height ; his complexion swarthy ; the muscles of his face, being relaxed, give him the appearance of a man of fifty years of age, nor can he be much younger ; his countenance has a faithful expression of great good humour and hilarity ; while his black eyes—that unerring index—possess an irradiating spirit, which proclaims the imperial powers of the mind that sits enthroned within.

This extraordinary man, without the aid of fancy, without the advantages of person, voice, attitude, gesture, or any of the ornaments of an orator, deserves to be considered as one of the most eloquent men in the world ; if eloquence may be said to consist in the power of seizing the attention with irresistible force, and never permitting it to elude the grasp, until the hearer has received the conviction which the speaker intends.

As to his person, it has already been described. His voice is dry, and hard; his attitude, in his most effective orations, was often extremely awkward; as it was not unusual for him to stand with his left foot in advance, while all his gesture proceeded from his right arm, and consisted merely in a vehement, perpendicular swing of it, from about the elevation of his head, to the bar, behind which he was accustomed to stand.

As to fancy, if she hold a seat in his mind at all, which I very much doubt, his gigantic genius tramples with disdain, on all her flower-decked plats and blooming parterres. How then, you will ask, with a look of incredulous curiosity, how is it possible that such a man can hold the attention of an audience enchained, through a speech of even ordinary length? I will tell you.

He possesses one original, and, almost, supernatural faculty; the faculty of developing a subject by a single glance of his mind, and detecting at once, the very point on which every controversy depends. No matter what the question: though ten times more knotty than " the gnarled oak," the lightning of heaven is not more rapid nor more resistless, than his astonishing penetration. Nor does the exercise of it seem to cost him an effort. On the contrary, it is as easy as vision. I am persuaded that his eyes do not fly over a landscape and take in its various objects with more promptitude and facility, than his mind embraces and analyzes the most complex subject.

Possessing while at the bar this intellectual elevation, which enabled him to look down and comprehend the whole ground at once, he determined immediately and without difficulty, on which side the question might be most advantageously approached and assailed. In a bad cause his art consisted in laying his premises so remotely from the point directly in debate, or else in terms so general and so specious, that the hearer, seeing no consequence which could be drawn from them, was just as willing to admit them as not; but his premises once admitted, the demonstration, however distant, followed as certainly, as cogently, as inevitably, as any demonstration in Euclid.

All his eloquence consists in the apparently deep self-conviction, and emphatic earnestness of his manner; the correspondent simplicity and energy of his style; the close and logical connexion of his thoughts; and the easy gradations by which he opens his lights on the attentive minds of his hearers.

The audience are never permitted to pause for a moment. There is no stopping to weave garlands of flowers, to hang in festoons, around a favourite argument. On the contrary, every sentence is progressive; every idea sheds new light on the subject; the listener is kept perpetually in that sweetly pleasurable vibration, with which the mind of man always receives new truths; the dawn advances in easy but unremitting peace; the subject opens gradually on the view; until, rising in high relief, in all its native colours and proportions, the argument is consummated, by the conviction of the delighted hearer.

The success of this gentleman has rendered it doubtful with several literary characters in this country, whether a high fancy be of real use or advantage to any one but a poet. They contend, that although the most beautiful flights of the happiest fancy, interspersed through an argument, may give an audience the momentary delightful swell of admiration, the transient thrill

of divinest rapture; yet, that they produce no
lasting effect in forwarding the purpose of the
speaker: on the contrary, that they break the
unity and disperse the force of an argument,
which otherwise, advancing in close array, like
the phalanx of Sparta, would carry every thing
before it. They give an instance in the celebrated Curran; and pretend that his fine fancy,
although it fires, dissolves and even transports his
audience to a momentary frenzy, is a real and a
fatal misfortune to his clients; as it calls off the
attention of the jurors from the intrinsic and
essential merits of the defence; eclipses the justice of the client's cause, in the blaze of the advocate's talents; induces a suspicion of the guilt
which requires such a glorious display of reful-
gence to divert the inquiry; and substitutes a
fruitless short-lived ecstasy, in the place of permanent and substantial conviction. Hence, they
say, that the client of Mr. Curran is, invariably,
the victim of the prosecution, which that able
and eloquent advocate is employed to resist.

The doctrine, in the abstract, may be true,
or, as doctor Doubty says, it may not be true;
for the present, I will not trouble you with the
expression of my opinion. I fear however, my
dear S . . . . . ., that Mr. Curran's failures may

be traced to a cause very different from any fault either in the style or execution of his enchanting defences : a cause . . . . . . but I am forgetting that this letter has yet to cross the Atlantic.*

To return to the . . . . of the United States. His political adversaries allege that he is a mere lawyer; that his mind has been so long trammelled by judicial precedent, so long habituated to the quart and tierce of forensic digladiation, (as doctor Johnson would probably have called it,) as to be unequal to the discussion of a great question of state. Mr. Curran, in his defence of Rowan, seems to have sanctioned the probability of such an effect from such a cause, when he complains of his own mind as having been narrowed and circumscribed, by a strict and technical adherence to established forms; but in the next breath, an astonishing burst of the grandest thought, and a power of comprehension to which there seems to be no earthly limit, proves that his complaint, as it relates to himself, is entirely without foundation.

Indeed, if the objection to . . . . mean any thing more than that he has not had

* The sentiment, which is suppressed, seems to wear the livery of Bedford, Moria, and the Prince of Wales.

the same illumination and exercise in matters
of state as if he had devoted his life to them, I
am unwilling to admit it. The force of a cannon is the same, whether pointed at a rampart
or a man of war, although practice may have
made the engineer more expert in the one case
than in the other. So it is clear, that practice
may give a man a greater command over one
class of subjects than another; but the innerent
energy of his mind remains the same, whither-
soever it may be directed. From this impression
I have never seen any cause to wonder at what
is called a universal genius : it proves only that
the man has applied a powerful mind to the
consideration of a great variety of subjects, and
pays a compliment rather to his superior industry, than his superior intellect. I am very certain that the gentleman of whom we are speaking, possesses the *acumen* which might constitute
him a universal genius, according to the usual
acceptation of the phrase. But if he be the
truant, which his warmest friends represent him
to be, there is very little probability that he will
ever reach this distinction.

Think you, my dear S . . . . . ., that the
two gentlemen, whom I have attempted to por-
tray to you, were, according to the notion of

Helvetius, born with equal minds; and that accident or education has produced the striking
difference which we perceive to exist between
them? I wish it were the case; and that the
. . . . would be pleased to reveal to
us, by what accident, or what system of education, he has acquired his peculiar sagacity and
promptitude. Until this shall be done, I fear I
must consider the hypothesis of Helvetius as a
splendid and flattering dream.

But I tire you:—adieu, for the present, friend
and guardian of my youth.

LETTER VI.

Jamestown, September 27.

I HAVE taken a pleasant ride of sixty miles down the river, in order, my dear S . . . . , to see the remains of the first English settlement in Virginia.

The site is a very handsome one. The river is three miles broad ; and, on the opposite shore, the country presents a fine range of bold and beautiful hills. But I find no vestiges of the ancient town, except the ruins of a church steeple, and a disordered group of old tombstones. On one of these, shaded by the boughs of a tree, whose trunk has embraced and grown over the edge of the stone, and seated on the head-stone of another grave, I now address you.

What a moment for a lugubrious meditation among the tombs ! but fear not ; I have neither the temper nor the genius of a Hervey ; and, as much as I revere his pious memory, I cannot envy him the possession of such a genius and such a temper. For my own part, I would not have suffered the mournful pleasure of writing

his book, and Doctor Young's Night Thoughts,
for all the just fame which they have both gained
by those celebrated productions. Much rather
would I have danced and sung, and played the
fiddle with Yorick, through the whimsical pages
of Tristram Shandy : that book which every
body justly censures and admires alternately;
and which will continue to be read, abused and
devoured, with ever fresh delight, as long as the
world shall relish a joyous laugh, or a tear of
the most delicious feeling.

By the by, here on one side is an inscription
on a gravestone, which would constitute no bad
theme for an occasional meditation from Yorick
himself. The stone, it seems, covers the grave of
a man who was born in the neighbourhood of
London ; and his epitaph concludes the short and
rudely executed account of his birth and death, by
declaring him to have been " a great sinner, in
hopes of a joyful resurrection ;" as if he had sin-
ned with no other intention, than to give himself
a fair title to these exulting hopes. But awk-
wardly and ludicrously as the sentiment is
expressed, it is in its meaning most just and
beautiful ; as it acknowledges the boundless
mercy of Heaven, and glances at that divinely
consoling proclamation, " come unto me, all

ye who are weary and heavy laden, and I
will give you rest."

The ruin of the steeple is about thirty feet
high, and mantled, to its very summit, with
ivy. It is difficult to look at this venerable
object, surrounded as it is with these awful
proofs of the mortality of man, without exclaiming in the pathetic solemnity of our
Shakspeare,

> " The cloud-capt towers, the gorgeous palaces,
> The solemn temples, the great globe itself,
> Yea, all which it inherits, shall dissolve;
> And, like this insubstantial pageant faded,
> Leave not a wreck behind."

Whence, my dear S . . . . . , arises the irrepressible reverence and tender affection with
which I look at this broken steeple? Is it that
my soul, by a secret, subtile process, invests
the mouldering ruin with her own powers;
imagines it a fellow being; a venerable old
man, a Nestor, or an Ossian, who has witnessed and survived the ravages of successive
generations, the companions of his youth, and
of his maturity, and now mourns his own solitary and desolate condition, and hails their
spirits in every passing cloud? Whatever
may be the cause, as I look at it, I feel my

soul drawn forward, as by the cords of gen-
tlest sympathy, and involuntarily open my lips
to offer consolation to the drooping pile.

Where, my S . . . . . , is the busy, bustling
crowd which landed here two hundred years
ago? Where is Smith, that pink of gallantry,
that flower of chivalry? I fancy that I can
see their first, slow and cautious approach to
the shore; their keen and vigilant eyes piercing the forest in every direction, to detect the
lurking Indian, with his tomahawk, bow and
arrow. Good Heavens! what an enterprise!
how full of the most fearful perils! and yet
how entirely profitless to the daring men who
personally undertook and achieved it! Through
what a series of the most spirit-chilling hard-
ships, had they to toil! How often did they
cast their eyes to England in vain! and with
what delusive hopes, day after day, did the
little, famished crew strain their sight to catch
the white sail of comfort and relief! But day
after day, the sun set, and darkness covered
the earth; but no sail of comfort or relief
came. How often in the pangs of hunger,
sickness, solitude and disconsolation, did they
think of London; her shops, her markets
groaning under the weight of plenty; her

streets swarming with gilded coaches, bustling
hacks, with crowds of lords, dukes and commons, with healthy, busy, contented faces of
every description ; and among them none more
healthy or more contented, than those of their
ungrateful and improvident directors ! But now
—where are they, all ? the little, famished colony which landed here, and the many-coloured
crowd of London—where are they, my dear
S. . . . . . ? Gone, where there is no distinction ; consigned to the common earth. Another
generation succeeded them : which, just as
busy and as bustling as that which fell before
it has sunk down into the same nothingness,
Another and yet another billow has rolled on,
each emulating its predecessor in height ; towering for its moment, and curling its foaming
honours to the clouds ; then roaring, breaking,
and perishing on the same shore.

Is it not strange, that, familiarly and universally as these things are known, yet each generation is as eager in the pursuit of its earthly
objects, projects its plans on a scale as extensive
as and laborious in their execution, with a spirit
as ardent and unrelaxing, as if this life and this
world were to last for ever ? It is, indeed, a
most benevolent interposition of Providence,

that these palpable and just views of the vanity
of human life are not permitted entirely to crush
the spirits, and unnerve the arm of industry.
But at the same time, methinks, it would be
wise in man to permit them to have, at least,
so much weight with him, as to prevent his
total absorption by the things of this earth,
and to point some of his thoughts and his
exertions, to a system of being, far more permanent, exalted and happy. Think not this
reflection too solemn. It is irresistibly inspired
by the objects around me ; and, as rarely as
it occurs, (much too rarely,) it is most certainly
and solemnly true, my S . . . . . .

It is curious to reflect, what a nation, in the
course of two hundred years, has sprung up
and flourished from the feeble, sickly germ
which was planted here ! Little did our short-
sighted court suspect the conflict which she
was preparing for herself; the convulsive throe
by which her infant colony would in a few
years burst from her, and start into a political
importance that would astonish the earth.

But Virginia, my dear S . . . . . ., as rapidly
as her population and her wealth must continue
to advance, wants one most important source
of solid grandeur; and that, too, the animating

soul of a republic.   I mean, public spirit; that sacred *amor patriæ* which filled Greece and Rome with patriots, heroes and scholars.

There seems to me to be but one object throughout the state; *to grow rich:* a passion which is visible, not only in the walks of private life, but which has crept into and poisoned every public body in the state.   Indeed, from the very genius of the government, by which all the public characters are, at short periodical elections, evolved from the body of the people, it cannot but happen, that the councils of the state must take the impulse of the private propensities of the country.   Hence, Virginia exhibits no great public improvements; hence, in spite of her wealth, every part of the country manifests her sufferings, either from the penury of her guardians, or their want of that attention and noble pride, wherewith it is their duty to consult her appearance.   Her roads and highways are frequently impassable, sometimes frightful; the very few public works which have been set on foot, instead of being carried on with spirit, are permitted to languish and pine and creep feebly along, in such a manner, that the first part of an edifice grows grey with age, and almost tumbles in ruins, before the

last part is lifted from the dust; highest offi-
cers are sustained with so avaricious, so niggardly a hand, that if they are not driven to
subsist on roots, and drink ditch-water, with
old Fabricius, it is not for the want of republican economy in the projectors of the salaries;
and, above all, the general culture of the human mind, that best cure for the aristocratic
distinctions which they profess to hate, that
best basis of the social and political equality,
which they profess to love: this culture, instead
of becoming a national care, is intrusted merely
to such individuals, as hazard, indigence, misfortunes or crimes, have forced from their
native Europe to seek an asylum and bread
in the wilds of America.

They have only one public seminary of
learning: a college in Williamsburg, about
seven miles from this place, which was erected
in the reign of our William and Mary, derives
its principal support from their munificence,
and therefore very properly bears their names.
This college, in the fastidious folly and affectation of republicanism, or what is worse, in
the niggardly spirit of parsimony which they
dignify with the name of economy, these democrats have endowed with a few despicable

fragments of surveyors' fees, &c., thus convert-
ing their national academy into a mere *laza-
retto*, and feeding its polite, scientific, and
highly respectable professors, like a band of
beggars, on the scraps and crumbs that fall
from the financial table.   And, then, instead of
aiding and energizing the police of the college,
by a few civil regulations, they permit their
youth to run riot in all the wildness of dissipation ; while the venerable professors are
forced to look on, in the deep mortification of
conscious impotence, and see their care and
zeal requited, by the ruin of their pupils and
the destruction of their seminary.

These are points which, at present, I can
barely touch ; when I have an easier seat and
writing desk, than a grave and a tombstone, it
will give me pleasure to dilate on them ; for, it
will afford an opportunity of exulting in the
superiority of our own energetic monarchy,
over this republican body without a soul.*

For the present, my dear S . . . ., I bid
you adieu.

---

* British insolence!   Yet it cannot be denied, however
painful the admission, that there is some foundation for his
censures.

LETTER VII.

Richmond, October 10.

I HAVE been, my dear S......., on an ex-
cursion through the countries which lie along
the eastern side of the Blue Ridge.   A general
description of that country and its inhabitants
may form the subject of a future letter.   For
the present, I must entertain you with an account of a most singular and interesting adventure, which I met with, in the course of the
tour.

It was one Sunday, as I travelled through
the county of Orange, that my eye was caught
by a cluster of horses tied near a ruinous, old,
wooden house, in the forest, not far from the
road side.   Having frequently seen such objects before, in travelling through these states,
I had no difficulty in understanding that this
was a place of religious worship.

Devotion alone should have stopped me, to
join in the duties of the congregation ; but I
must confess, that curiosity, to hear the preacher
of such a wilderness, was not the least of my

motives.   On entering, I was struck with his preternatural appearance, he was a tall and very spare old man; his head, which was covered with a white linen cap, his shrivelled hands, and his voice, were all shaking under the influence of a palsy; and a few moments ascertained to me that he was perfectly blind.

The first emotions which touched my breast, were those of mingled pity and veneration. But ah! sacred God! how soon were all my feelings changed!   The lips of Plato were never more worthy of a prognostic swarm of bees, than were the lips of this holy man!   It was a day of the administration of the sacrament; and his subject, of course, was the passion of our Saviour.   I had heard the subject handled a thousand times : I had thought it exhausted long ago.   Little did I suppose, that in the wild woods of America, I was to meet with a man whose eloquence would give to this topic a new and more sublime pathos, than I had ever before witnessed.

As he descended from the pulpit, to distribute the mystic symbols, there was a peculiar, a more than human solemnity in his air and manner which made my blood run cold, and my whole frame shiver.

He then drew a picture of the sufferings of our Saviour; his trial before Pilate; his ascent up Calvary; his crucifixion, and his death. I knew the whole history; but never, until then, had I heard the circumstances so selected, so arranged, so coloured! It was all new: and I seemed to have heard it for the first time in my life. His enunciation was so deliberate, that his voice trembled on every syllable; and every heart in the assembly trembled in unison. His peculiar phrases had that force of description that the original scene appeared to be, at that moment, acting before our eyes. We saw the very faces of the Jews: the staring, frightful distortions of malice and rage. We saw the buffet; my soul kindled with a flame of indignation; and my hands were involuntarily and convulsively clinched.

But when he came to touch on the patience, the forgiving meekness of our Saviour; when he drew, to the life, his blessed eyes streaming in tears to heaven; his voice breathing to God, a soft and gentle prayer of pardon on his enemies, "Father, forgive them, for they know not what they do"—the voice of the preacher, which had all along faltered, grew fainter and fainter, until his utterance being entirely ob-

structed by the force of his feelings, he raised
his handkerchief to his eyes, and burst into a
loud and irrepressible flood of grief. The effect
is inconceivable. The whole house resounded with the mingled groans, and sobs, and
shrieks of the congregation.

It was some time before the tumult had
subsided, so far as to permit him to proceed.
Indeed, judging by the usual, but fallacious
standard of my own weakness, I began to be
very uneasy for the situation of the preacher.
For I could not conceive, how he would be
able to let his audience down from the height
to which he had wound them, without impair-
ing the solemnity and dignity of his subject,
or perhaps shocking them by the abruptness
of the fall. But—no; the descent was as
beautiful and sublime, as the elevation had been
rapid and enthusiastic.

The first sentence, with which he broke the
awful silence, was a quotation from Rousseau,
" Socrates died like a philosopher, but Jesus
Christ, like a God !"

I despair of giving you any idea of the effect
produced by this short sentence, unless you
could perfectly conceive the whole manner of
the man, as well as the peculiar crisis in the

discourse. Never before, did I completely
understand what Demosthenes meant by laying such stress on *delivery*. You are to bring
before you the venerable figure of the preacher ;
his blindness, constantly recalling to your
recollection old Homer, Ossian and Milton, and
associating with his performance, the melancholy grandeur of their geniuses ; you are to
imagine that you hear his slow, solemn, well-
accented enunciation, and his voice of affecting, trembling melody ; you are to remember
the pitch of passion and enthusiasm to which
the congregation were raised ; and then, the
few minutes of portentous, death-like silence
which reigned throughout the house ; the
preacher removing his white handkerchief from
his aged face, (even yet wet from the recent
torrent of his tears,) and slowly stretching forth
the palsied hand which holds it, begins the
sentence, " Socrates died like a philosopher"—
then pausing, raising his other hand, pressing
them both clasped together, with warmth and
energy to his breast, lifting his " sightless
balls" to heaven, and pouring his whole soul
into his tremulous voice—" but Jesus Christ—
like a God !" If he had been indeed and in

truth an angel of light, the effect could scarcely have been more divine.

Whatever I had been able to conceive of the sublimity of Massillon, or the force of Bourdaloue, had fallen far short of the power which I felt from the delivery of this simple sentence. The blood, which just before had rushed in a hurricane upon my brain, and, in the violence and agony of my feelings, had held my whole system in suspense, now ran back into my heart, with a sensation which I cannot describe —a kind of shuddering delicious horror! The paroxysm of blended pity and indignation, to which I had been transported, subsided into the deepest self-abasement, humility and adoration. I had just been lacerated and dissolved by sympathy, for our Saviour as a fellow creature; but now, with fear and trembling, I adored him as—" a God !"

If this description give you the impression, that this incomparable minister had any thing of shallow, theatrical trick in his manner, it does him great injustice. I have never seen, in any other orator, such a union of simplicity and majesty. He has not a gesture, an attitude or an accent, to which he does not seem forced, by the sentiment which he is expressing. His mind is too serious, too earnest, too solicitous, and, at the same time, too dignified, to stoop to artifice. Although as far removed from ostentation as a man can be, yet it is clear from the train, the style and substance of his thoughts, that he is, not only a very polite scholar, but a man of extensive and profound erudition. I was forcibly struck with a short, yet beautiful character which he drew of our learned and amiable countryman, Sir Robert Boyle: he spoke of him, as if " his noble mind had, even before death, divested herself of all influence from his frail tabernacle of flesh ;" and called him, in his peculiarly emphatic and impressive manner, " a pure intelligence : the link between men and angels."

This man has been before my imagination almost ever since. A thousand times, as I rode along, I dropped the reins of my bridle, stretched forth my hand, and tried to imitate his quotation from Rousseau ; a thousand times I abandoned the attempt in despair, and felt persuaded that his peculiar manner and power arose from an energy of soul, which nature could give, but which no human being could justly copy. In short, he seems to be altogether a being of a former age, or of a totally different nature from the rest of men. As I recall, at this moment, several of his awfully striking attitudes, the chilling tide, with which my blood begins to pour along my arteries, reminds me of the emotions produced by the first sight of Gray's introductory picture of his bard :

> " On a rock, whose haughty brow,
>   Frowns o'er old Conway's foaming flood,
> Robed in the sable garb of wo,
>   With haggard eyes the poet stood ;
> (Loose his beard and hoary hair
>   Streamed, like a meteor, to the troubled air :)
> And with a poet's hand and prophet's fire,
>   Struck the deep sorrows of his lyre."

Guess my surprise, when, on my arrival at Richmond, and mentioning the name of this man, I found not one person who had ever before heard of *James Waddell!!* Is it not strange, that such a genius as this, so accomplished a scholar, so divine an orator, should be permitted to languish and die in obscurity, within eighty miles of the metropolis of Virginia? To me it is a conclusive argument, either that the Virginians have no taste for the highest strains of the most sublime oratory, or that they are destitute of a much more important quality, the love of genuine and exalted religion.

Indeed, it is too clear, my friend, that this soil abounds more in weeds of foreign birth, than in good and salubrious fruits. Among others, the noxious weed of infidelity has struck a deep, a fatal root, and spread its pestilential branches far around. I fear that our eccentric and fanciful countryman, Godwin, has contributed not a little to water and cherish this pernicious exotic. There is a novelty, a splendour, a boldness in his scheme of morals, peculiarly fitted to captivate a youthful and ardent mind. A young man feels his delicacy flattered, in the idea of being emancipated from the old, obsolete and vulgar motives of moral conduct; and acting correctly from motives quite new, refined and sublimated in the crucible of pure, abstracted reason. Unfortunately, however, in this attempt to change the motives of his conduct, he loses the old ones, while the new, either from being too etherial and sublime, or from some other want of congeniality, refuse to mix and lay hold of the gross materials of his nature. Thus he becomes emancipated indeed; discharged not only from ancient and vulgar shackles; but

also, from the modern, finespun, tinselled re-
straints of his divine Godwin. Having imbibed the high spirit of literary adventure, he
disdains the limits of the moral world; and
advancing boldly to the throne of God, he
questions him on his dispensations, and
demands the reasons of his laws. But the
counsels of heaven are *above* the ken, *not
contrary to* the voice of human reason; and
the unfortunate youth, unable to reach and
measure them, recoils from the attempt, with
melancholy rashness, into infidelity and deism.
Godwin's glittering theories are on his lips.
Utopia or Mezorania, boast not of a purer
moralist, *in words*, than the young Godwin-
ian; but the unbridled licentiousness of *his
conduct* makes it manifest, that if Godwin's
principles be true in the abstract, they are not
fit for this system of things; whatever they
might be in the republic of Plato.

From a life of inglorious indolence, by far
too prevalent among the young men of this
country, the transition is easy and natural to
immorality and dissipation. It is at this
giddy period of life, when a series of dissolute
courses have debauched the purity and innocence of the heart, shaken the pillars of the

understanding, and converted her sound and wholesome operations into little more than a set of feverish starts and incoherent and delirious dreams; it is in such a situation that a new-fangled theory is welcomed as an amusing guest, and deism is embraced as a balmy comforter against the pangs of an offended conscience. This coalition, once formed and habitually consolidated, "farewell, a long farewell" to honour, genius and glory! From such a gulf of complicated ruin, few have the energy even to attempt an escape. The moment of cool reflection, which should save them, is too big with horror to be endured. Every plunge is deeper, until the tragedy is finally wound up by a pistol or a halter. Do not believe that I am drawing from fancy: the picture is unfortunately true. Few dramas, indeed, have yet reached their catastrophe; but, too many are in a rapid progress toward it.

These thoughts are affecting and oppressive. I am glad to retreat from them, by bidding you adieu; and offering my prayers to heaven, that you may never lose the pure, the genial consolations of unshaken faith, and an approving conscience. Once more, my dear S . . . ., adieu.

LETTER VIII.

Richmond, October 15.

MEN of talents in this country, my dear S . . . ., have been generally bred to the profession of the law ; and indeed, throughout the United States, I have met with few persons of exalted intellect, whose powers have been directed to any other pursuit. The bar, in America is the road to honour ; and hence, although the profession is graced by the most shining geniuses on the continent, it is incumbered also by a melancholy group of young men, who hang on the rear of the bar, like Goethe's sable clouds in the western horizon. I have been told that the bar of Virginia was, a few years ago, pronounced by the supreme court of the United States, to be the most enlightened and able on the continent. I am very incompetent to decide on the merit of their legal acquirements ; but, putting aside the partiality of a Briton, I do not think either of the gentlemen by any means so eloquent or

so erudite as our countryman Erskine.   With
your permission, however, I will make you
better acquainted with the few characters who
lead the van of the profession.

Mr. . . . . has great personal advantages.
A figure large and portly ; his features uncom-
monly fine ;   his dark eyes and his whole
countenance lighted up with an expression of
the most conciliating sensibility ; his attitudes
dignified and commanding ; his gesture easy
and graceful ; his voice perfect harmony ; and
his whole manner that of an accomplished
and engaging gentleman.   I have reason to
believe that the expression of his countenance
does no more than justice to his heart.   If I
be correctly informed, his feelings are exquisite ;
and the proofs of his benevolence are various
and clear beyond the possibility of doubt.   He
has filled the highest offices in this commonwealth and has very long maintained a most
respectable rank in his profession.   His character, with the people, is that of a great lawyer
and an eloquent speaker ; and, indeed, so many
men of discernment and taste entertain this
opinion, and my prepossessions in his favour
are so strong, on account of the amiable qualities of his character, that I am very well dis-

posed to doubt the accuracy of my own judgment as it relates to him.

To me, however, it seems, that his mind, as
is often but not invariably the case, corres-
ponds with his personal appearance : that is,
that it is turned rather for ornament than for
severe use : *pompæ, quam pugnæ aptior*, as
Tully expresses it.   His speeches, I think,
deserve the censure which lord Verulam pro-
nounces on the writers posterior to the reform-
ation of the church.   " Luther," says he,
" standing alone, against the church of Rome,
found it necessary to awaken all antiquity in
his behalf : this introduced the study of the dead
languages, a taste for the fulness of the Cice-
ronean manner ; and hence the still prevalent error of hunting more after words than
matter, and more after the choiceness of the
phrase and the round and clean composition of the sentence, and the sweet fallings
of the clauses, and the varying and illustration
of their works with tropes and figures, than
after the weight of matter, worth of subject,
soundness of argument, life of invention, or
depth of judgment."

Mr. . . . . . . 's temper and habits lead him to
the swelling, stately manner of Bolingbroke;

but either from the want of promptitude and richness of conception, or his too sedulous concern and "hunting after words," he does not maintain that manner, smoothly and happily. On the contrary, the spirits of his hearers, after having been awakened and put into sweet and pleasant motion, have their tide, not unfrequently checked, ruffled and painfully obstructed by the hesitation and perplexity of the speaker. It certainly must demand, my dear S . . . . . . , a mind of very high powers to support the swell of Bolingbroke, with felicity. The tones of voice, which naturally belong to it, keep the expectation continually " on tiptoe," and this must be gratified not only by the most oily fluency, but by a course of argument clear as light, and an alternate play of imagination as grand and magnificent as Herschell's dance of the sidereal system. The work requires to be perpetually urged forward. One interruption in the current of the language, one poor thought or abortion of fancy, one vacant aversion of the eye, or relaxation in the expression of the face, entirely breaks and dissolves the whole charm. The speaker, indeed, may go on and evolve, here and there, a pretty thought; but the wondrous magic of the whole is gone for ever.

Whether it be from any defect in the organization of Mr. . . . .'s mind, or that his passion for the fine dress of his thoughts is the master passion, which, "like Aaron's serpent, swallows up the rest," I will not undertake to decide ; but perhaps it results from one of those two causes, that all the arguments, which I have ever heard from him, are defective in that important and most material character, the *lucidus ordo*.

I have been sometimes inclined to believe, that a man's division of his argument would be generally found to contain a secret history of the difficulties which he himself has encountered in the investigation of his subject. I am firmly persuaded that the extreme prolixity of many discourses to which we are doomed to listen, is chargeable, not to the fertility, but to the darkness and impotence of the brain which produces them. A man, who sees his object in a strong light, marches directly up to it, in a right line, with the firm step of a soldier; while another, residing in a less illumined zone, wanders and reels in the twilight of the brain, and ere he attain his object, treads a maze as intricate and perplexing as that of the celebrated labyrinth of Crete.

It was remarkable of the . . . . of the United States, whom I mentioned to you in a former letter as looking through a subject at a single glance, that he almost invariably seized one strong point only, the pivot of the controversy; this point he would enforce with all his powers, never permitting his own mind to waver, nor obscuring those of his hearers, by a cloud of inferior, unimportant considerations. But this is not the manner of Mr. . . . . I suspect, that in the preparatory investigation of a subject, he gains his ground by slow and laborious gradations; and that his difficulties are numerous and embarrassing. Hence it is, perhaps, that his points are generally too multifarious; and although, among the rest, he exhibits the strong point, its appearance is too often like that of Issachar, "bow'd down between two burthens." I take this to be a very ill-judged method. It may serve indeed to make the multitude stare; but it frustrates the great purpose of the speaker. Instead of giving a simple, lucid and animated view of a subject, it overloads, confounds and fatigues the listener. Instead of leaving him under the vivacity of

clear and full conviction, it leaves him bewil-
dered, darkling, asleep; and when he awakes,
he

> ———" wakes, emerging from a sea of dream
> Tumultuous; where his wreck'd, desponding thought,
> From wave to wave of wild uncertainty,
> At random drove,—her helm of reason lost."

I incline to believe that if there be a blemish
in the mind of this amiable gentleman, it is
the want of a strong and masculine judgment.
If such an agent had wielded the sceptre of
his understanding, it is presumable, that, ere
this, it would have chastised his exuberant
fondness for literary finery, and the too ostentatious and unfortunate parade of points in his
argument, on which I have just commented.
If I may confide in the replies which I have
heard given to him at the bar, this want of
judgment is sometimes manifested in his
selection and application of law cases. But of
this I can judge only from the triumphant air
with which his adversaries seize his cases and
appear to turn them against him.

He is certainly a man of close and elaborate
research.   It would seem to me, however, my
dear S . . . . , that in order to constitute a
scientific lawyer, something more is necessary

than the patient and persevering revolution of the leaves of the author. Does it not require a discernment sufficiently clear and strong to eviscerate the principles of each case; a judgment potent enough to digest, connect and systematize them, and to distinguish, at once, in any future combination of circumstances, the very feature which gives or refuses to a principle, a just application? Without such intellectual properties, I should conjecture, (for on this subject I can only conjecture,) that a man could not have the fair advantage and perfect command of his reading. For, in the first place, I should apprehend, that he would never discover the application of a case, without the recurrence of all the same circumstances; in the next place, that his cases would form a perfect chaos, a *rudis indigestaque moles*, in his brain; and lastly, that he would often and sometimes perhaps fatally mistake the identifying feature, and furnish his antagonist with a formidable weapon against himself.

But let me fly from this entangled wilderness, of which I have so little knowledge, and return to Mr. . . . . . Although when brought to the standard of perfect oratory, he may be subject to the censures which I have passed

on him ; yet it is to be acknowledged, and I
make the acknowledgment with pleasure,
that he is a man of extensive reading, a well-
informed lawyer, a fine *belles lettres* scholar,
and sometimes a beautiful speaker.

The gentleman who has been pointed out
to me as holding the next if not an equal grade
in the profession, is Mr. . . . . . He is, I am
told, upwards of forty years of age; but his
look, I think, is more juvenile. As to stature,
he is about the ordinary height of men ; his
form genteel, his person agile. He is distinguished by a quickness of look, a sprightly
step, and that peculiarly jaunty air, which I
have heretofore mentioned, as characterizing
the people of New-York. It is an air, however,
which, (perhaps, because I am a plain son of
John Bull,) is not entirely to my taste. Striking, indeed, it is ; highly genteel, and calculated for *eclat ;* but then, I fear, that it may be
censured as being to artificial : as having,
therefore, too little appearance of connexion
with the heart; too little of that amiable simplicity, that winning softness, that vital warmth,
which I have felt in the manner of a certain
friend of mine. This objection, however, is
not meant to touch his heart. I do not mean

to censure his sensibility or his virtues. The remark applies only to the mere exterior of *his manners;* and even the censure which I have pronounced on *that,* is purely the result of a different taste, which is, at least, as probably wrong as that of Mr. . . . . . .

Indeed, my dear S . . . . . ., I have seen few eminent men in this or any other country, who have been able so far to repress the exulting pride of conscious talents, as to put on the behaviour which is calculated to win the hearts of the people. I mean that behaviour, which steers between a low-spirited, cringing sycophancy and ostentatious condescension on the one hand, and a haughty self-importance and supercilious contempt of one's fellow creatures on the other; that behaviour, in which, while a man displays a just respect for his own feelings and character, he seems, nevertheless, to concentre himself with the disposition and inclination of the person to whom he speaks; in a word, that happy behaviour, in which versatility and candour, modesty and dignity, are sweetly and harmoniously tempered and blended. Any Englishman, but yourself, my S . . . . ., would easily recognize the original from which this latter picture is drawn.

This leads me off from the character of Mr. . . . . . ., to remark a moral defect, which I have several times observed in this country. Many well meaning men, having heard much of the hollow, ceremonious professions and hypocritical grimace of courts; disgusted with every thing which savours of aristocratic or monarchic parade; and smitten with the love of republican simplicity and honesty; have fallen into a ruggedness of deportment, a thousand times more proud, more intolerable and disgusting, than Shakspeare's foppish lord, with his chin new reaped and pouncet box. They scorn to conceal their thoughts; and in the expression of them confound bluntness with honesty. Their opinions are all *dogmas*. It is perfectly immaterial to them what any one else may think. Nay, many of them seem to have forgotten, that others can think, or feel at all. In pursuit of the haggard phantom of republicanism,* they dash on, like Sir Joseph Banks, giving chase to the emperor of Morocco, regardless of the sweet and tender blossoms of sensibility, which fall and bleed, and

* This phrase is scarcely excusable, even in a Briton and a lord.

die behind them.   What an error is this, my
dear S . . . . ! I am frequently disposed to
ask such men, "think you, that the stern and
implacable Achilles was an honester man than
the gentle, humane and considerate Hector?
Was the arrogant and imperious Alexander an
honester man than the meek, compassionate,
and amiable Cyrus? Was the proud, the rough,
the surly Cato, more honest than the soft,
polite and delicate Scipio Africanus? In short,
are not honesty and humanity compatible?
And what is the most genuine and captivating
politeness, but humanity refined?"

But to return from this digression.   The
qualities, by which Mr. . . . . strikes the multitude, are his ingenuity and his wit.   But
those, who look more closely into the anatomy
of his mind, discover many properties of much
higher dignity and importance.   This gentleman, in my opinion, unites in himself a greater
diversity of talents and acquirements, than any
other at the bar of Virginia.   He has the reputation, and I doubt not a just one, of possessing much legal science.   He has an exquisite
and a highly cultivated taste for polite literature; a genius quick and fertile; a style pure
and classic; a stream of perspicuous and beau-

tiful elocution; an ingenuity which no difficulties can entangle or embarrass; and a wit,
whose vivid and brilliant coruscation, can gild
and decorate the darkest subject. He chooses
his ground, in the first instance with great
judgment; and when, in the progress of a
cause, an unexpected evolution of testimony,
or intermediate decisions from the bench, have
beaten that ground from under him, he possesses a happy, an astonishing versatility, by
which he is enabled at once, to take a new
position, without appearing to have lost an
atom, either in the measure or stability of his
basis. This is a faculty which I have observed before in an inferior degree; but
Mr. . . . . . is so adroit, so superior in the execution of it, that in him it appears a new and
peculiar talent; his statements, his narrations,
his arguments, are all as transparent as the
light of day. He reasons logically, and de-
claims very handsomely. It is true, he never
brandishes the Olympic thunder of Homer,
but then he seldom, if ever, sinks beneath the
chaste and attractive majesty of Virgil.

His fault is, that he has not veiled his ingenuity with sufficient address. Hence, I am
told, that he is considered as a Proteus; and the

courts are disposed to doubt their senses even
when he appears in his proper shape.   But in
spite of this adverse and unpropitious distrust,
M . . . . . .'s popularity is still in its flood ; and
he is justly considered as an honour and an
ornament to his profession.

Adieu, my friend, for the present.   Ere long
we may take another tour through this gallery
of portraits, if more interesting objects do not
call us off.   Again, my S . . . . . ., good night.

LETTER IX.

Richmond, October 30.

TALENTS, my dear S . . . . . , wherever they
have had a suitable theatre, have never failed
to emerge from obscurity and assume their
proper rank in the estimation of the world.
The celebrated Camden is said to have been
the tenant of a garret. Yet from the darkness,
poverty and ignominy, of this residence, he
advanced to distinction and wealth, and graced
the first offices and titles of our island. It is
impossible to turn over the British biography,
without being struck and charmed by the multitude of correspondent examples ; a venerable
group of *novi homines*, as the Romans called
them ; men, who, from the lowest depths of
obscurity and want, and without even the influence of a patron, have risen to the first
honours of their country, and founded their
own families anew. In every nation, and in
every age, great talents, thrown fairly into the
point of public observation, will invariably pro-

duce the same ultimate effect. The jealous pride of power may attempt to repress and crush them; the base and malignant rancour of impotent spleen and envy may strive to embarrass and retard their flight; but these efforts, so far from achieving their ignoble purpose, so far from producing a discernible obliquity in the ascent of genuine and vigorous talents, will serve only to increase their momentum and mark their transit with an additional stream of glory.

When the great earl of Chatham first made his appearance in our house of commons, and began to astonish and transport the British parliament, and the British nation, by the boldness, the force and range of his thoughts, and the celestial fire and pathos of his eloquence, it is well known, that the minister Walpole, and his brother Horace, (from motives very easily understood,) exerted all their wit, all their oratory, all their acquirements of every description, sustained and enforced by the unfeeling "insolence of office," to heave a mountain on his gigantic genius, and hide it from the world. Poor and powerless attempt! The tables were turned. He rose upon them in the might and irresistible energy of his genius; and in spite of all their convolutions, frantic agonies and spasms, he strangled them and their whole faction with as much ease as Hercules did the serpent ministers of jealousy that were sent to assail his infant cradle. Who can turn over the debates of the day, and read the account of this conflict between youthful ardour and hoary headed cunning and power, without kindling in the cause of the tyro, and shouting at his victory? That they should have attempted to pass off the grand, yet solid and judicious operations of a mind like his, as being mere theatrical start and emotion; the giddy, hair-brained eccentricities of a romantic boy! That they should have had the presumption to suppose themselves capable of chaining down to the floor of the parliament, a genius so ethereal, towering, and sublime! Why did they not, in the next breath, by way of crowning the climax of vanity, bid the magnificent fire-ball to descend from its exalted and appropriate region, to perform its splendid tour along the surface of the earth?*

---

* See a beautiful note in Darwin's Botanic Garden, in which the writer suggests the probability of three concentric strata of our atmosphere, in which, or between them, are produced four kinds of meteors; in the lowest, the com-

When the son of this great man too, our present minister and his compeer and rival, our friend, first commenced their political career, the public papers teemed with strictures on their respective talents; the first was censured as being merely a dry and even a flimsy reasoner; the last was stigmatized as an empty declaimer.   But error and misrepresentation soon expire, and are forgotten; while truth rises upon their ruins, and " flourishes in eternal youth."   Thus, the false, the light, fugacious newspaper criticisms, which attempted to dissect and censure the arrangement of those gentlemen's talents, have been long since swept away by the besom of oblivion.   They wanted truth, that soul, which alone can secure immortality to any literary

---

mon lightning; in the next, shooting stars; and the highest region, which he supposes to consist of inflammable gas tenfold ligher than the common atmospheric air, he makes the theatre of the northern light, and fireball or draco volans. He recites the history of one of the latter, seen in the year 1758, which was estimated to have been a mile and a half in circumference; to have been one hundred miles high; and to have moved toward the north, thirty miles in a second. It had a real tail, many miles long, which threw off sparks in its course; and the whole exploded with a sound like that of distant thunder.—*Bot. Garden, Part* 1, *Note* 1.

work. And Mr. Pitt and Mr. Fox have for many years been reciprocally and alternately recognized, just as their subject demands it, either as close and cogent reasoners, or as beautiful and superb rhetoricians.

Talents, therefore, which are before the public, have nothing to dread, either from the jealous pride of power, or from the transient misrepresentations of party, spleen, or envy. In spite of opposition from any cause, their buoyant spirit will lift them to their proper grade : it would be unjust that it should lift them higher.

It is true, there always are, and always will be, in every society, individuals, who will fancy themselves examples of genius overlooked, underrated, or invidiously oppressed. But the misfortune of such persons is imputable to their own vanity, and not to the public opinion, which has weighed and graduated them.

We remember many of our schoolmates, whose geniuses bloomed and died within the walls of *Alma Mater ;* but whose bodies still live, the moving monuments of departed splendour, the animated and affecting remembrances of the extreme fragility of the human intellect. We remember others, who have entered on public life with the most exulting promise; have flown from the earth, like rockets ; and, after a short and brilliant flight, have bursted with one or two explosions—to blaze no more. Others, by a few premature scintillations of thought, have led themselves and their partial friends, to hope that they were fast advancing to a dawn of soft and beauteous light, and a meridian of bright and gorgeous effulgence ; but their day has never yet broken ; and never will it break. They are doomed for ever to that dim, crepuscular light, which surrounds the frozen poles, when the sun has retreated to the opposite circle of the heavens. Theirs is the eternal glimmering of the brain ; and their most luminous displays are the faint twinklings of the glow-worm. We have seen others, who, at their start, gain a casual projectility, which rises them above their proper grade ; but by the just operation of their specific gravity, they are made to subside again, and settle ultimately in the sphere to which they properly belong.

All these characters, and many others who have had even slighter bases for their once sanguine, but now blasted hopes, form a quer-

ulous and melancholy band of moonstruck de-
claimers against the injustice of the world, the
agency of envy, the force of destiny, &c.,
charging their misfortune on every thing but
the true cause : their own want of intrinsic
sterling merit; their want of that copious,
perennial spring of great and useful thought,
without which a man may hope in vain for
growing reputation. Nor are they always
satisfied with wailing their own destiny, pouring out the bitterest imprecations of their souls
on the cruel stars which presided at their
birth, and aspersing the justice of the public
opinion which has scaled them : too often in
the contortions and pangs of disappointed ambition, they cast a scowling eye over the
world of man; start back and blanch at the
lustre of superior merit; and exert all the
diabolical incantations of their black art, to
conjure up an impervious vapour, in order to
shroud its glories from the world. But it is
all in vain. In spite of every thing, the public opinion will finally do justice to us all.
The man who comes fairly before the world,
and who possesses the great and vigorous
stamina which entitle him to a *nich* in the
temple of glory, has no reason to dread the

ultimate result; however slow his progress
may be, he will in the end most indubitably
receive that distinction. While the rest, " the
swallows of science," the butterflies of genius,
may flutter for their spring ; but they will soon
pass away and be remembered no more. No
enterprising man, therefore, (and least of all
the truly great man,) has reason to droop or
repine at any efforts which he may suppose
to be made with the view to depress him ;
since he may rely on the universal and un-
changing truth, that talents, which are before
the world, will most inevitably find their pro-
pér level ; and this is, certainly, all that a just
man should desire. Let, then, the tempest of
envy or of malice howl around him. His
genius will consecrate him ; and any attempt
to extinguish that, will be as unavailing as
would a human effort " to quench the stars."

I have been led further into these reflections
than I had anticipated. The train was started
by casting my eyes over Virginia ; observing
the very few who have advanced on the theatre of public observation, and the very many
who will remain for ever behind the scenes.

What frequent instances of high, native
genius have I seen springing in the wilder-

nesses of this country; genius, whose blossoms the light of science has never courted
into expansion; genius, which is doomed to
fall and die, far from the notice and the haunts
of men! How often, as I have held my way
through the western forests of this state, and
reflected on the vigorous shoots of superior
intellect, which were freezing and perishing
there for the want of culture; how often have
I recalled the moment, when our pathetic
Gray, reclining under the mouldering elm of
his country churchyard, while the sigh of
genial sympathy broke from his heart, and
the tear of noble pity started in his eye, exclaimed,

> "Perhaps in this neglected spot is laid
>   Some heart once pregnant with celestial fire,
> Hands that the rod of empire might have sway'd,
>   Or wak'd to ecstacy the living lyre.
>
> But knowledge to their eyes, her ample page,
>   Rich with the spoils of time, did ne'er unroll;
> Chill penury repress'd their noble rage,
>   And froze the genial current of their soul.
>
> Full many a gem of purest ray serene,
>   The dark, unfathom'd caves of ocean bear;
> Full many a flower is born to blush unseen,
>   And waste its sweetness on the desert air.

Some village Hampden, that with dauntless breast,
  The little tyrant of his fields withstood;
Some mute, inglorious Milton, here may rest;
  Some Cromwell, guiltless of his country's blood.

Th' applause of list'ning senates to command,
  The threats of pain and ruin to despise,
To scatter plenty o'er a smiling land,
  And read their history in a nation's eyes.

Their lot forbade"—

The heart of a philanthropist, no matter to
what country or what form of government he
may belong, immediately inquires, "And is
there no mode to prevent this melancholy
waste of talents? Is there no mode by which
the rays of science might be so diffused over
the state, as to call forth each latent bud into
life and luxuriance?" There is such a mode :
and what renders the legislature of this state
still more inexcusable, the plan by which these
important purposes might be effected, has been
drawn out and has lain by them for nearly
thirty years. The declaration of the independence of this commonwealth was made in
the month of May, 1776.* In the fall of that

---

* This is a fact which the public journals of the state
established beyond controversy; although the legal process

year, a statute, or, as it is called here, " an act
of assembly," was made, providing that a
committee of five persons should be appointed
to prepare a code of laws, adapted to the change
of the state government. This code was to
be submitted to the legislature of the country,
and to be ratified or rejected by their suffrage.

In the ensuing November, by a resolution
of the same legislature, Thomas Jefferson,
Edmund Pendleton, George Wythe, George
Mason and Thomas Ludwell Lee, esquires,
were appointed a committee to execute the
work in question. It was prepared by the
three first named gentlemen; the first of them
now the President of the United States; the
second, the president of the supreme court of
appeals of Virginia, and the third, the judge of
the high court of chancery at this place.

I have perused this system of state police
with admiration. It is evidently the work of
minds of most astonishing greatness; capable,
at once, of a grand, profound and comprehensive survey of the present and future interest

and other public acts of Virginia modestly waive this pre-
cedence, and date the foundation of the commonwealth on
the 4th of July, 1776, the day on which the declaration of the
independence of the United States was promulged.

and glory of the whole state; and of pursuing that interest and glory through all the remote and minute ramifications of the extensive and elaborate detail.

Among other wise and highly patriotic bills which are proposed, there is one for the more general diffusion of knowledge. After a pre-amble, in which the importance of the subject to the republic is most ably and eloquently announced, the bill proposes a simple and beautiful scheme, whereby science (like justice under the institutions of our Alfred) would have been "carried to every man's door." Genius, instead of having to break its way through the thick opposing clouds of native obscurity, indigence and ignorance, was to be sought for through every family in the commonwealth; the sacred spark, wherever it was detected, was to be tenderly cherished, fed and fanned into a flame; its innate properties and tendencies were to be developed and examined, and then cautiously and judiciously invested with all the auxiliary energy and radiance of which its character was susceptible.

What a plan was here to give stability and solid glory to the republic! If you ask me why it has never been adopted, I answer, that as a foreigner, I can perceive no possible reason for it, except that the comprehensive views and generous patriotism which produced the bill, have not prevailed throughout the country, nor presided in the body on whose vote the adoption of the bill depended. I have new reason to remark it, almost every day, that there is throughout Virginia, a most deplorable destitution of public spirit, of the noble pride and love of country. Unless the body of the people can be awakened from this fatal apathy; unless their thoughts and their feelings can be urged beyond the narrow confines of their own private affairs; unless they can be strongly inspired with the public zeal, the *amor patriæ* of the ancient republics, the national embellishment, and the national grandeur of this opulent state, must be reserved for very distant ages.

Adieu, my S . . . . . .; perhaps you will hear from me again before I leave Richmond.

AN APOLOGY

IN REPLY TO A HINT.

THE letters of the British Spy were furnished
to amuse the citizens of the town and country,
and not to give pain to any one human being.
Accordingly, nothing has been said in censure
of the integrity, the philanthropy, benevolence,
charity, or any other moral or religious virtue
or grace of any one Virginian, who has been
introduced into those letters.   Nothing, indeed,
could be justly said on those heads, in censure
of either of the gentlemen.   It is true, that
some letters have been published, which have
attempted to analyze the *minds* of three or four
well known citizens of this state, and in order
to designate them more particularly, a description of the *person* and *manner* of each gentleman was given.   This has been called "throwing stones at other people's glass houses," and
the person who has communicated those letters
(gratuitously styled their " author") is politely
reminded that he himself resides " in a glass
house."

If this be correctly understood, it implies a threat of *retaliation ;* but all that the laws of *retaliation* could justify, would be to amuse the town and country with a description of the *person, manner* and *mind* of the author (as he is called) of the British Spy. He fears, however, that it would puzzle the hinter, whatever his genius may be, to render so barren a subject interesting and amusing to the public; and he would be much obliged to the hinter if he could make it appear that he (the furnisher of the letters) deserves to be drawn into comparison, either as to person, manner, or mind, with any one of the gentlemen delineated by the British Spy.   As to his person, indeed, he is less solicitous ; the defects of that were imposed on him by nature ; and there is no principle better established than this general principle of eternal truth and justice, that no man ought to be censured for the contingencies over which he had no controul. As to his manner, he has as little objection to a public description of that as his person.

To save the trouble of others, however, he relinquishes all pretensions either to the striking elegance which is calculated to excite admiration and respect, or to the conciliating grace

and vital warmth which are qualified to gain
enthusiastic friends. His manner is probably
such as would be produced, nine times out of
ten, by the rustic education to which he was
exposed.

As to his mind, it is almost such as nature
made it. He cannot boast with Gray, that
"science frowned not on his humble birth."
But what of this? A man may very accurately
anatomize the powers of a mind far superior
to his own. It is not improbable Zoilus's criticisms of Homer were just; since every nod of
Homer's was a fair subject of criticism. Yet
who will suppose that Zoilus would have produced such a work as the Iliad? It is impossible to read Dennis's criticisms of Addison's
Cato without being forcibly struck with their
justice, and wondering that they have never
before occurred to ourselves. Yet there is no
man, who will therefore pronounce the genius
of Dennis equal to that of Addison. These
facts are so palpable and so well understood,
that the person who furnished the letters of the
British Spy (even if he had been their author)
could scarcely have had the presumption to
suppose, nor, I trust, the injustice to desire, that
the public would pronounce his mind free

from the defects, much less indued with the energies and beauties of those which he criticises.

But where is the harm which has been done? Who are the gentlemen introduced into the British Spy? Are they young men just emerging into notice, and concerning whom the public have yet to form an opinion? Far from it. They are gentlemen, who have long been, and who still are displaying themselves in the very centre of the circle of general observation. They have not hid their light under a bushel. Their city is built on a high hill. There is not a feature of their persons, nor a quality of their mind or manner, which has not been long and well known, and remarked, commented on, criticised, repeated and reiterated a thousand and ten thousand times in every circle and every corner of the country.

Was it in the power, then, of any remarks in an anonymous and fugitive newspaper publication, either to injure or serve gentlemen so well and so eminently known? On the contrary, if those remarks were untrue, they would be instantaneously and infallibly corrected by the public opinon and knowledge of the subject; if the remarks were true, they would add no new fact to the public opinion and the public knowledge. Thinking thus, nothing was more distant, either from the expectation or wish of the person who has furnished the press with the letters of the British Spy, than that he was about to do an injury to the character, or to inflict a wound on the feelings of any citizen of the country. Why could he have expected or wished any such effect? He could not have been actuated by resentment; for neither of those gentlemen have ever done him an injury. He could not have been moved by personal interest; since his conscious inferiority, as well as the nature of his pursuits, remove him far from the possibility of being ever brought into collision with either of those gentlemen. He could not have been impelled by diabolical envy, or the malicious agony of blasted ambition; since his country has already distinguished him far, very far, beyond his desert. And of the malevolence of heart which could intentionally do a wicked, a wanton and unprovoked injury, he is persuaded that either of the gentlemen, if they knew him, would most freely and cheerfully acquit him.

If he be asked why he published the letters describing those characters? He answers,

First, For the same reason that he would, if he could, present to the town a set of landscape paintings, representing all the lovely prospects which belong to their beautiful city; to furnish them with the amusement and pleasure which arise from surveying an accurate picture of a well known original: and this implies, that he could not have believed himself adding new information as to the originals themselves.

Secondly, He hoped that the abstracted and miscellaneous remarks, which were blended with the description of those characters, might not be without their use to the many literary young men who are growing up in Virginia.

If the letters of the British Spy have gone beyond these purposes; if they have given pain to the gentlemen described; (for as to doing them an injury, it is certainly out of the question,) there is no man in the community disposed to regret it more sensibly than the man who furnished those letters for publication.

But while honour and justice compel the writer of this article to give these explanations, and make these acknowledgments to the gentlemen immediately interested, he begs he may not be considered as descending to the meanness of begging mercy on his own "glass house." On the contrary, the person who has published the polite hint in question, is welcome to commence his assault as soon as he pleases. He can scarcely point out one defect in the person, manner, or mind of this writer, of which he is not already conscious. And if he meant by his menace any thing more; if he meant to insinuate a suspicion to the public, that the honesty, integrity, or moral purity, of the man who furnished the letters of the British Spy for publication, are assailable on any ground of truth; if such was his intention he has intended an injury, at which this writer laughs in proud security; an injury, for which his own heart, if it be a good one, will not forgive him so soon, as will the heart of the man whom he has attempted to injure.

The writer of this article tenders in return this hint to the hinter; that before he commences his hostile operations, he will be sure of his man. As to the person who really did furnish the British Spy—the finger of conjecture has been erroneously pointed at several who reside in this state. It would be unjust and barbarous to punish the innocent for the guilty, if guilt can be justly charged on the British Spy.

LETTER X.

Richmond, December 10.

In one of my late rides into the surrounding
country, I stopped at a little inn to refresh myself and my horse; and, as the landlord was
neither a Boniface, nor "mine host of the gar-
ter," I called for a book, by way of killing time,
while the preparations for my repast were going
forward. He brought me a shattered fragment
of the second volume of the Spectator, which
he told me was the only book in the house, for
" he never troubled his head about reading;"
and by way of conclusive proof, he further
informed me, that this fragment, the only book
in the house, had been sleeping unmolested in
the dust of his mantel-piece, for ten or fifteen
years. I could not meet my venerable countryman, in a foreign land, and in this humiliating
plight, nor hear of the inhuman and gothic
contempt with which he had been treated,
without the liveliest emotion. So I read my
host a lecture on the subject, to which he
appeared to pay as little attention as he had

before done to the Spectator; and, with the
sang froid of a Dutchman, answered me in
the cant of the country, that he "had other fish
to fry," and left me.

It had been so long since I had had an opportunity of opening that agreeable collection,
that the few numbers which were now before
me, appeared almost entirely new; and I cannot
describe to you, the avidity and delight with
which I devoured those beautiful and interesting speculations.

Is it not strange, my dear S . . . ., that
such a work should have ever lost an inch of
ground? A style so sweet and simple, and yet
so ornamented! a temper so benevolent, so
cheerful, so exhilarating! a body of knowledge,
and of original thought, so immense and various! so strikingly just, so universally useful!
What person, of any age, sex, temper, calling,
or pursuit, can possibly converse with the
Spectator, without being conscious of immediate improvement?

To the spleen, he is as perpetual and never-
failing an antidote, as he is to ignorance and
immorality. No matter for the disposition of
mind in which you take him up; you catch, as
you go along, the happy tone of spirits which

prevails throughout the work; you smile at
the wit, laugh at the drollery, feel your mind
enlightened, your heart opened, softened and
refined; and when you lay him down, you are
sure to be in a better humour, both with yourself and every body else. I have never mentioned the subject to a reader of the Spectator,
who did not admit this to be the invariable
process; and in such a world of misfortunes,
of cares, and sorrows, and guilt, as this is, what
a prize would this collection be, if it were rightly
estimated!

Were I the sovereign of a nation, which
spoke the English language, and wished my
subjects cheerful, virtuous and enlightened, I
would furnish every poor family in my dominions (and see that the rich furnished themselves) with a copy of the Spectator; and
ordain that the parents or children should read
four or five numbers, aloud, every night in the
year. For one of the peculiar perfections of
the work is, that while it contains such a mass
of ancient and modern learning, so much of
profound wisdom, and of beautiful composition,
yet there is scarcely a number throughout the
eight volumes, which is not level to the
meanest capacity. Another perfection is, that

the Spectator will never become tiresome to
any one whose taste. and whose heart remain
uncorrupted.

I do not mean that this author should be
read to the exclusion of others ; much less that
he should stand in the way of the generous
pursuit of science, or interrupt the discharge of
social or private duties. All the counsels of the
work itself have a directly reverse tendency.
It furnishes a store of the clearest argument
and of the most amiable and captivating ex-
hortations, " to raise the genius, and to mend
the heart." I regret, only, that such a book
should be thrown by, and almost entirely forgotten, while the gilded blasphemies of infidels,
and "the noontide trances" of penicious theorists, are hailed with rapture, and echoed around
the world. For such, I should be pleased to
see the Spectator universally substituted : and,
throwing out of the question its morality, its
literary information, its sweetly contagious
serenity, and the pure and chaste beauties of
its style ; and considering it merely as a curiosity, as concentring the brilliant sports of the
finest cluster of geniuses that ever graced the
earth, it surely deserves perpetual attention,
respect and consecration.

There is, methinks, my S . . . . ., a great
fault in the world, as it respects this subject:
a giddy instability, a light and fluttering vanity,
a prurient longing after novelty, an impatience,
a disgust, a fastidious contempt of every thing
that is old. You will not understand me as
censuring the progress of sound science. I am
not so infatuated an antiquarian, nor so poor a
philanthropist, as to seek to retard the expansion
of the human mind. But I lament the eternal
oblivion into which our old authors, those
giants of literature, are permitted to sink, while
the world stands open-eyed and open-mouthed
to catch every modern, tinselled abortion as it
falls from the press. In the polite circles of
America, for instance, perhaps there is no want of
taste, and even zeal, for letters. I have seen several gentlemen who appear to have an accurate,
a minute acquaintance with the whole range of
literature, in its present state of improvement:
yet, you will be surprised to hear, that I have
not met with more than one or two persons in
this country, who have ever read the works of
Bacon or of Boyle. They delight to saunter
in the upper story, sustained and adorned, as it
is, with the delicate proportions, the foliage and
flourishes of the Corinthian order; but they

disdain to make any acquaintance, or hold communion at all, with the Tuscan and Doric plainness and strength which base and support the whole edifice.

As to lord Verulam, when he is considered as the father of experimental philosophy; as the champion, whose vigour battered down the idolized chimeras of Aristotle, together with all the appendant and immeasurable webs of the brain, woven and hung upon them, by the ingenious dreamers of the schools; as the hero who not only rescued and redeemed the world from all this darkness, jargon, perplexity and error; but, from the stores of his own great mind, poured a flood of light upon the earth, straightened the devious paths of science, and planned the whole paradise, which we now find so full of fragrance, beauty and grandeur; when he is considered, I say, in these points of view, I am astonished that literary gentlemen do not court his acquaintance, if not through reverence, at least through curiosity. The person who does so will find every period filled with pure and solid golden bullion: that bullion, which several much admired posterior writers have merely moulded into various forms,

or beaten into leaf, and taught to spread its
floating splendours to the sun.

This insatiate palate for novelty which I have
mentioned, has had a very striking effect on
the style of modern productions. The plain
language of easy conversation will no longer
do. The writer who contends for fame, or
even for truth, is obliged to consult the reigning
taste of the day. Hence too often, in opposition to his own judgment, he is led to encum-
ber his ideas with a gorgeous load of ornaments; and when he would present to the
public a body of pure, substantial and useful
thought, he finds himself constrained to encrust
and bury its utility within a dazzling case; to
convert a feast of reason into a concert of
sounds: a rich intellectual boon into a mere
bouquet of variegated pinks and blushing roses.
In his turn he contributes to establish and
spread wider the perversion of the public taste;
and thus, on a principle resembling that of
action and reaction, the author and the public
reciprocate the injury; just as, in the licentious
reign of our Charles the 2d, the dramatist
and his audience were wont to poison each
other.

A history of style would indeed be a curious and highly interesting one : I mean a philosophical, as well as chronological history; one which, beside marking the gradations, changes and fluctuations exhibited in the style of different ages and different countries, should open the regular or contingent causes of all those gradations, changes and fluctuations.   I should be particularly pleased to see a learned and penetrating mind employed on the question: Whether the gradual adornment, which we observe in a nation's style, result from the progress of science ; or whether there be an infancy, a youth, and a manhood, in a nation's sensibility, which rising in a distant age, like a newborn billow, rolls on through succeeding generations, with accumulating height and force, and bears along with it the concurrent expression of that sensibility, until they both swell and tower into the sublime—and sometimes break into the *bathos*.

The historical facts, as well as the metaphysical consideration of the subject, perplex these questions extremely ; and, as Sir Roger de Coverly says, "much may be said on both sides."   For the present I shall say nothing on either ; except that from some of Mr. Blair's remarks, it would seem that neither of those hypotheses will solve the phenomenon before us. If I remember his opinion correctly, the most sublime style is to be sought in a state of nature; when, anterior to the existence of science, the scantiness of a language forces a people to notice the points of resemblance between the great natural objects with which they are surrounded; to apply to one the terms which belong to another; and thus, by compulsion, to rise at once into simile and metaphor, and launch into all the boldness of trope and figure. If this be true, it would seem that the progress of a civilized nation toward sublimity of style is perfectly a retrograde manœuvre: that is, that they will be sublime according to the nearness of their approach to the primeval state of nature.

This is a curious, and to me, a bewitching subject. But it leads to a volume of thought, which is not to be condensed in a letter. I will remark only one extraordinary fact as it relates to style. The Augustan age is pronounced by some critics to have furnished the finest models of style, embellished to the highest endurable point; and of this, Cicero is always adduced as the most illustrious example.

Yet it is remarkable, that seventy or eighty years afterwards, when the Roman style had become much more luxuriant, and was denounced by the critics of the day* as having transcended the limits of genuine ornament, Pliny, the younger, in a letter to a friend, thought it necessary to enter into a formal vindication of three or four metaphors, which he had used in an oration, and which had been censured in Rome for their extravagance ; but which, by the side of the meanest of Curran's figures, would be poor, insipid and flat. Yet who will say that Curran's style has gone beyond the point of endurance ? Who is not pleased with its purity ? Who is not ravished by its sublimity.

In England, how wide is the chasm between the style of Lord Verulam and that of Edmund Burke, or M'Intosh's introduction to his *Vindicæ Gallicæ!* That of the first is the plain dress of a Quaker ; that of the two last the magnificent paraphernalia of Louis XIV. of France. In lord Verulam's day, his style was distinguished for its superior ornament ; and in this respect, it was thought impossible to sur-

---

* See Quinctillian's Institutes.

pass it.   Yet Mr. Burke, Mr. M'Intosh, and the
other *fine* writers of the present age, have, by
contrast, reduced lord Verulam's flower garden
to the appearance of a simple culinary square.

Perhaps it is for this reason, and because, as
you know, I am an epicure, that I am very
much interested by lord Verulam's manner.
It is indeed a most agreeable relief to my mind
to turn from the stately and dazzling rhapsodies of the day, and converse with this plain
and sensible old gentleman.   To me his style
is gratifying on many accounts; and there is
this advantage in him, that instead of having
three or four ideas rolled over and over again,
like the fantastic evolutions and ever-changing
shapes of the same sun-embroidered cloud, you
gain new materials, new information at every
breath.

Sir Robert Boyle is, in my opinion, another
author of the same description, and therefore
an equal, if not a higher favourite with me.
In point of ornament he is the first grade in
the mighty space, (through the whole of which
the gradations may be distinctly traced,) between
Bacon and Burke.   Yet he has no redundant
verbiage; has about him a perfectly patriarchal
simplicity; and every period is pregnant with

matter. He has this advantage too over lord Verulam ; that he not only investigates all the subjects which are calculated to try the clearness, the force and the comprehension of the human intellect : he introduces others also, in handling of which he shows the masterly power with which he could touch the keys of the heart, and awaken all the tones of sensibility which belong to man. Surely, if ever a human being deserved to be canonized for great, unclouded intelligence, and seraphic purity and ecstasy of soul, that being was Sir Robert Boyle.

When I reflect that this "pure intelligence, this link between men and angels," was a Christian, and look around upon the petty infidels and deists with which the world swarms, I am lost in amazement ! Have they seen arguments against religion, which were not presented to Sir Robert Boyle? His religious works show that they have not. Are their judgments better able to weigh those arguments than his was? They have not the vanity even to believe it. Is the beam of their judgments more steady, and less liable to be disturbed by passion than his? No ; for in this he seems to have excelled all mankind. Are their minds more elevated and more capable of comprehending the whole of this great subject, with all its connexions and dependencies, than was the mind of Sir Robert Boyle? Look at the men: and the question is answered. How then does it happen that they have been conducted to a conclusion so perfectly the reverse of his? It is for this very reason; because their judgments are less extricated from the influence and raised above the mists of passion: it is because their minds are less ethereal and comprehensive; less capable than his was "to look through nature up to nature's God." And let them hug their precious, barren, hopeless infidelity: they are welcome to the horrible embrace! May we, my friend, never lose the rich and inexhaustible comforts of religion. Adieu, my S . . . . .

THE author of " An Inquirer" on the theory
ᶠ the earth, begs leave to offer the following
observations to the publisher of " the British
Spy," in answer to some of his additional
notes.

When the Inquirer read, in the second letter
of the British Spy, that "the perpetual revolution of the earth, from west to east, has the obvious tendency to conglomerate the loose sands of
the sea on the eastern coast,"—"that whether
the rolling of the earth to the east give to the
ocean an actual counter-current to the west
or not, the newly emerged pinnacles are
whirled, by the earth's motion, through the
waters of the deep;" and from the continued
operation of the causes which produced them,
that " all continents and islands will be caused,
reciprocally to approximate ;" when he read
these and other similar passages, he saw no
reason to doubt, that the British Spy considered
the ocean *now*, as well as formerly, affected by
the rotation of the earth; or, to express the

same thing more correctly, that the rotatory motion of the earth is but partially communicated
to the ocean. This opinion, which a thousand
facts may be brought to disprove, and which
the favourite cosmogonist of the British Spy
says* no man can entertain who has the least
knowledge of physics, it was decorous to suppose, had been advanced from inadvertence.
If the meaning of the writer were taken by the
Inquirer in a greater latitude than was meant,
he is not the less sorry for his mistake, because
it was not a natural one, and was not confined
to himself.

But the annotator of the Spy, without saying whether the supposed current now exist or
not, thinks the *former* existence of such a current not improbable, and puts a case by way
of illustrating his hypotheses. My reasoning
on the subject, somewhat different from his, is
briefly this:

If the whole surface of the earth, when it
first received its rotatory impulse, were covered
with water, *and this impulse were communi-*

---

* The passage in Smellie's translation of Buffon stands
thus: but every man who has the least knowledge of physics, must allow, that no fluid which surrounds the earth,
can be affected by its rotation.— *Vol. I. On Regular Winds.*

cated to its solid part alone, then, indeed, a current to the west would be produced; and would continue, until the resistance, occasioned by the friction of the waters, gradually communicated the whole motion of the earth to the ocean. It is not easy to say, when this current would cease; but it seems to me it would be more likely to wear the bed of the ocean smooth, than to raise protuberances; and even, though it were to cause sand banks, it could never elevate them above its own level.

I should observe that, to avoid circumlocution, I admit a *current of the west;* because the effect is the same, as to alluvion, whether the earth revolve under the waters, or the waters roll over the earth; though the fact is, that the ocean, like the oil in the plate, in the experiment proposed, would have a tendency to remain at rest, and whatever motion it acquired, must be *to the east,* like that of the earth from which it was derived.

If we suppose a few solitary mountains to lift their heads above the circumfluous ocean, we may infer, by the rules of strict analogy, that they would be worn away by the friction of the passing waters, rather than that they would receive any accessions of soil.

But let us suppose some ridges of mountains running from north to south, and of sufficient extent and elevation to obstruct the course of the waters. In this case, the sudden whirling of the earth to the east would force the ocean on its western shores, where it would accumulate, until the gravity of the mass thus elevated, overcome the force which raised it. Then one vast undulation of the stupendous mass would take place, from shore to shore, and would continue until it gradually yielded to the united effect of friction and gravity. A comparison between vessels of different sizes, partly filled with water, might enable us to form a rational conjecture of the term of this oscillation; but be it in one year, or many years, I think the effect would more probably be, an abrasion of the mountain, than the formation of a continent.

But the *postulatum*, that the first impulse to the earth was communicated to its solid part alone, on which all these suppositions rest, is but a possibility: whether we suppose that the cause, which first whirled the earth on its axis, is an ascending link in nature's chain of causes, or the immediate act of the first Great Cause of all, it is not unlikely that it penetrated and influenced every particle of matter, whether it were solid, liquid or æriform.

On this subject, our suppositions are to be limited only by our invention. One man may resort to electricity, according to an alleged property of that fluid; another, to magnetism; a third, to the action of the sun's rays; and a fourth, to a quality inherent in matter; according to either of which hypotheses, no current could have existed.

Monsieur de Buffon, indeed, ascribes the earth's rotation to a mechanical and partial impulse, the *oblique* stroke of a comet; but as, according to him, the earth was then one entire globe of melted glass, its rotatory motion must have been uniform, long before the ocean existed.

Whoever would dispel the clouds in which this question is enveloped, and make it as clear "as the light of heaven," should indeed be *mihi magnus Apollo :* but hypotheses, of which nothing can be said, but that they are not impossible, though they may beguile the lounger of a heavy hour, are little likely to further our knowledge of nature. In so boundless a field of conjecture, with scarce one twinkling star to guide us, we can hardly hope to find, among the numberless tracts of error, that which singly leads to truth.

When the Inquirer spoke of the general *bouleversement* which many subterranean appearances indicated, he did not mean even to hint at their cause, but simply to express, as the word imports, the topsyturvy disorder, in which vegetable and marine substances are found; the one far *above*, and the other far *below*, the seat of its original production. At the moment he was attempting to show, that every explanation of these phenomena was imperfect and premature, he hardly would have ventured to give one himself; for though " we should not suffer ourselves to be passively fed on the pap of science," *when we have attained our maturity*, yet until we have attained it, he thinks it is better to be in leading-strings, than to stumble at every step.

In the progress of science, I doubt whether sound principles are abandoned for those that are less true. Novelty in moral speculation, aided as it may be, by our passions, may dazzle and mislead, but in physics, though one error may give place to another, when truth once gets possession, she holds it firm, ever after. Thus the theories of cosmogonists fol-

low one another, like wave obtruding upon
wave ; each demonstrating the fallacy of those
which went before, and proved absurd in turn ;
while the philosophy of Newton, in spite of
the continued opposition of French academi-
cians, and the later reveries of St. Pierre, gradually gains universal credit and respect. The
member of the Royal Society, who accounted
for the trade winds by the transpiration of
tropical sea-weed, may have had his admirers ;
but he has not been able to shake the theory of
Dr. Halley. If Harvey's system of generation
had been as well supported by facts, as his discovery of the circulation of the blood, all hostility to the one, as well as the other, would
have ended with his life.

It certainly is not philosophical "to discard
a theory," because it may be unsupported by
a name, nor yet because there are other more
recent theories. In these and many other
general remarks, I entirely concur with the
writer, though I do not clearly discern their
application.

I cannot conclude, without regretting, that I
should be compelled to differ with a writer
whose talents I so much admire, and whose
sentiments I so often approve ; but to borrow

a celebrated sentiment, my esteem for truth exceeds even my esteem for the British Spy. Though neither of us may chance to convince the other, yet, if our discussion should lead those who have not the same parental tenderness for particular hypotheses or doubts, to a better understanding of the subject, the light, that is thus elicited, will console me for the collision which produced it.

October 12, 1803.

THE END.